TRAIN
YOUR
BRAIN
FOR SUCCESS!

Ron Ball

Train Your Brain For Success

by Ron Ball

ISBN: 978-1-942991-77-9

Published by:

Editorial RENUEVO
www.EditorialRenuevo.com
info@EditorialRenuevo.com

Table of Contents

Introduction

When I was eight years old, my dad took me for a walk one sunny Saturday morning. I was more interested in the dog across the street than in my father's conversation, but I was happy we were together.

We had just passed the local Baptist church when we were hailed by a white-haired gentleman dressed in a business suit. I vaguely recognized the man but had never met him. He was shorter than my dad, and he bounced with energy. When we all arrived at the same spot on the sidewalk, my father began to talk with him.

After a few moments (I was still watching the dog, a friendly golden lab), I realized that my dad was motioning me toward the other man. "I want you to meet someone," he said.

The man in the suit surprised me. He knelt in front me, solemnly shook my hand, and asked my name. When I replied that my name was Ronnie, he smiled (a smile that made me think of Santa Claus) and said his name was Burl, and he was very happy to meet me. He asked me several simple questions, which I answered, and then he told me I could become anything I wanted if I had a purpose and was willing to work hard. With that, the man stood, spoke a moment longer with my father, and then continued on the sidewalk, waving as he walked away.

When the man disappeared from view, my dad

asked if I knew who he was. When I said no, my father explained that he was the owner of the local bank and the richest man in the community.

My dad then told me the story of how Burl, as a young man, had visited the local bank to secure a loan for his new business. The loan officer ridiculed young Burl and told him his ideas would not work. He rudely told Burl that the bank would not even consider his loan and told him to leave. What happened next is still legendary in the history of our small Kentucky town.

My dad said Burl stood in front of the other bank customers and boldly told the loan officer that one day he would be back, and he would own the bank. Burl did return, and when he did, it was as owner of the bank. That was the man who knelt on the sidewalk on a beautiful June morning, shook the hand of an eight-year-old boy, and told him he could accomplish his dreams.

I saw Burl many times over the years. He always remembered my name, always smiled his Santa Claus smile, and always asked if I was working hard to make my dreams come true.

That moment on the sidewalk with Burl Spurlock awakened in me a desire to understand success. I searched out why some people did great things while others walked a path of frustration and mediocrity. I wanted to know what made one individual push toward higher achievements while another spent his life in dull disappointment. I wanted to know how to win.

As I moved into adulthood, four important things happened:

1. I entered a dynamic relationship with Jesus Christ, which changed everything. It is still the foundation of my life.
2. I married my wife, Amy, who shared my excitement about personal success. She also encouraged me in my walk with God and my pursuit of worthy goals.
3. I fell in love with reading and research. I wanted to fill my mind with information that would make me a better person and help me become more effective.
4. I realized God had called me to introduce people to the Savior Jesus Christ to help them discover and experience His thrilling purpose for their lives. I sensed God had led me to such wonderful ideas about success because He wanted to use that research to bless and enrich other people and their families.

All the reading and hungry research I did eventually led me to the new frontier of brain science. The Bible says you are "fearfully and wonderfully made [by God]" (Psalm 139:14 New International Version), and that includes your brain. God gave you an instrument of power and possibility that is capable of unbelievable things. Your brain is incredible because of the amazing God who created it.

This book you are about to read is based on brain research. I am not a scientist, but I have studied several people who are. I have learned from them what I am about to present to you. I have used the insights in this book; I have tested and proven them to myself. So I offer them to you to bless and improve your life as they have mine.

Success is not easy. We need all the help we can get. When allowed to do so, there are parts of your brain that can help you in many ways. They can help you make better decisions, earn more money, and get out of debt; they can also help calm your stress and strengthen your relationships.

The chapters of this book are arranged in this way: The first three will teach you about your brain, and the remaining ones will teach you how to use your brain to create a *performance explosion* in your life and business.

Start now to discover the basics, and then learn how to train your brain to be your best friend. Use this book to unlock your brain's God-given potential.

Get ready to be amazed!

Chapter 1

The Brain

Can you find the common thread to all of these stories?

Jennifer rides what I call the romance rollercoaster—high, low, up and down. She keeps picking unsuitable guys. She becomes excited about a young man, absolutely convinced that he is the man of her dreams, and then the relationship crashes and burns within weeks or months. Jennifer is a nice, intelligent young woman; she is pleasant, fun to be around, a college graduate. But she has become a jerk magnet: she attracts the wrong guys—and the result is a series of broken hearts.

A young man named Todd lives in what I call the limbo of unfulfilled potential. He is a college graduate with big dreams, but he has had three jobs in seven years. He is twenty-nine years old, and he fears he is being sucked into an abyss with no way to escape. Todd's dreams were enormous when he got out of school; he wanted to rock his world. But now Todd is struggling to find the right corporate fit.

Logan and Stephanie have been married four and a half years. They have a beautiful daughter, Samantha, who is eleven months old. They are stuck in reruns of same night, same fight; they continually have the same arguments. When they married, they married with the dazzling dreams of eternal romance, excitement, companionship, sex, fun, and friendship. But the stresses of living (rearing their daughter and normal frustrations of life) have pushed them near the edge of dissatisfaction and disappointment.

Then there is forty-eight-year-old James, an outgoing man who has had a decent career in insurance, but who is living a life of diminishing returns. His future is getting smaller every year. He has to come up with more money just to maintain his social and economic position. James is tired, trapped, and frustrated. He wonders what he should do.

Richard is radically different because he has risen like a rocket. He has a happy family and plenty of income. He has maximum security even though he is only in his late thirties. He is in love with God, his life, and his church. Richard is climbing with no end in sight.

If you examine them (and I have because I know them), there is something fundamental to all these stories: the way they see life; the way they look at their circumstances.

Jennifer, for example, has a fairy tale image of romance. She is convinced that the right young man will magically appear and sweep her off her feet, and she will not have to do anything but just be herself.

Todd expects the managers of his different jobs to acknowledge his amazing abilities and promote him. Todd is a little angry that no one has recognized his capabilities. After all, people have been telling him that he has great potential since he was in junior high; his mom and dad sure told him. But Todd is waiting for other people to recognize his superior talents. He is thinking in a different way.

Logan and Stephanie have a high expectation of marriage. They both come from good families, with parents who are still happily married, so they waltzed into marriage expecting everything to be easy. They had their child (someone to show off and spoil at Christmas, they thought). They did not plan on diapers and bottles and sleepless nights and temper tantrums. They are unhappy because the way they think about marriage has not matched their reality.

James has always expected something to happen. He is a gambler; he is the guy who thinks, "My ship will come in; it will dock. This next year something will happen for me. This is my year." But he does nothing to make it happen. He pursues nothing different to alter his circumstances; but hey, that ship is on its way. He believes it, so he is now living a life of diminishing returns.

Richard is different from the others. He became a Christian several years ago; he loves God with all his heart. He reads motivational books and is committed to his family. Richard is very balanced and down-to-earth. He is not some head-in-the-clouds kind of guy who does not face truth. No, he is very levelheaded and faces difficulties head-on. He is good at what he does, a real man. Richard thinks life is an adventure to be lived. The way he thinks has demonstrated to him the way his life should be, and the way he thinks has resulted in the adventure he has pictured in his mind.

Six different people with six different lives. The way they view their circumstances affects their actions and their lives. Everything hinges on the way these people think.

At this point, you are probably wondering how you think. And you are asking me, "Ron, what's the big deal? I want to be prosperous. I want my family to work well. I want my career to move forward financially. I want to be spiritually content and emotionally satisfied." Just like these individuals I described, so much of your life depends on your thinking, on the way your brain operates.

Researchers Gillian Butler and Tony Hope recently came up with a fascinating list of five types of people and how they think about life. In their book, *Managing Your Mind: the Mental Fitness Guide*, they write that some people are sages. I know it sounds like a spice used in cooking; but in this case, it is an old term for a wise person, someone who seeks great depths of wisdom and understanding. The researchers say some people look at life through the eyes of a sage. These are people who seek knowledge, who may or may not be nerds. They are data-oriented and focused on finding out new information. They love to dig; they love to research.

Butler and Hope also point out a downside: Sages usually exhibit little or no action in their lives. They accumulate vast amounts of knowledge and enormous piles of information, but they do little with them. Sure, the sages can be very entertaining at a party and somewhat intimidating at dinner because they know so much. (They would be great at Trivial Pursuit or Jeopardy.) But sages rarely do all that much.

Butler and Hope then say that some people are what they call travelers: those who like new experiences and new things. I relate to this group because I love to travel. I have relaxed in little cafés on narrow side streets in Paris eating delicious Parisian food. I have sat at Chamonix in the French Alps, at the base of Mont Blanc (the tallest mountain in Western Europe), eating special cheese fondue with fresh bread baked in the chalet. I have eaten a prize-winning fish entrée in Melbourne, Australia. I have sampled the outdoor markets in Seoul, Korea. I appreciate the benefits and joys of travel.

But Butler and Hope are describing something more than a love of globe-trotting. The travelers they discuss do not actually need to travel, which makes them even more interesting. The people in this research are those who simply like new things. They love change; they crave experiences. They are experientialists, and they cannot get enough; they cannot enjoy life too much. They operate on the belief that the grass is always greener; they are always looking for more. Because of that, the travelers may lack roots; they may lack stability. These individuals can be so quick to try new things that sometimes it is hard for them to settle into a long-term commitment.

The drifters, another type Butler and Hope identify, are easy to picture because they are carried along by the currents. The drifters are those who graduate from high school, tech school, or college and accept the first job for which they applied. They drift at that job for years; they do not plan. They live for the weekends. They cannot wait to do something they enjoy: go out to eat, relax, or take in some sporting event. They drift along with no guidance or clear goals; they are OK with their life as it is. They feel no enormous excitement, no deep fulfillment; they drift with the currents of whatever they are involved in. The drifters also are susceptible to the fashion flow. They get caught up in the latest fashionable person, political leader, entertainer, or trend. They are captivated by the latest craze. The travelers want to experience new things all the time, but the drifters want new things because everybody else thinks they are cool. If someone says, "This is what everyone is doing," they will attach themselves to that fashion moment and drift until something else catches their attention.

The ostriches are another type the researches identify. In the natural world, ostriches are big, interesting birds. They cannot fly, but they have strong legs they use for running and for defending themselves. They have a powerful kick that is capable of killing a predator. I have seen ostriches at a game preserve in Australia where I made the mistake of trying to pet them. They were wild and crazy and a little dangerous. According to Butler and Hope, the ostrich people are the ones who hide from others; and if anyone gets too close to them, they will kick. They are the people who isolate themselves from others; they resist relationships even in their own families. And if someone gets too close, the ostrich-type will forcefully kick because they just want to be left alone.

The authors say that some people choose to be conductors of the orchestra. (Richard is a good example). And I love the word the researchers use: choose. These are the ones who decide to bring balance to their lives: God and family, money and wealth, achievement and relaxation. They decide to conduct their lives like an orchestra leader, with all parts coming together in harmony (in balance).

It is interesting that Butler and Hope and their five types of people are quoted in a book about brain activity. The whole purpose of breaking people down into groups of sages, travelers, drifters, ostriches, and orchestra conductors is to show how their different brains operate, how their minds view life, and how they conduct themselves mentally. Butler and Hope are convinced (as are other brain researchers) that people's lives are a result of how they think. Your life is a result of how you think. Now, I know there is more to it than that. I frequently refer to God; I refer to my relationship with Jesus Christ because it is the most important thing in the world to me. God is real; a relationship with Christ is real. Yes, there are mental (brain) aspects of behavior, but, I believe, there are also spiritual roots to behavior. God made your brain. He gave you all the ingredients you need to advance your life, but you have to understand how your brain produces your special personality. Who you are is a result of your experiences interacting with your brain. Once you understand how your brain sees your world, then you can use that knowledge to improve your odds of personal success and achievement.

Your physical brain contains your mind. Recent studies have revealed that your brain can be redirected, or retrained, which is why I titled this book, *Train Your Brain for Success*. I have studied over three thousand pages of scientific text researching for this book because I want to give you accurate information. Training your brain for success is a great idea, but how do you do it?

First, you need to understand your brain; you need to learn some facts. The typical human brain weighs about three pounds. "Does the size of my brain determine how smart I am?" you ask. Not necessarily. Albert Einstein's brain weighed 2.7 pounds, which is 10 percent smaller than the average person's brain. I think we all know what he accomplished in his life. So, brain size is not critical for your mental ability to succeed.

The brain is divided into two hemispheres (sides) and is about 80 percent water. Even though it represents approximately 2 percent of your body weight, it uses 20 percent of the body's energy, about 25 watts of electrical power continually.

Scientists used to think the brain was like a computer, but it is not. Your brain should be embarrassed to be compared to a computer because there is such a big difference. Researchers now think the brain is more like an ecosystem, a jungle of connective possibilities. One researcher referred to the brain as "a-ready-to-respond-to-your-environment machine."

Michael Roizen and Mehmet Oz are two medical doctors who have appeared on the Discovery Health Channel, the Oprah Winfrey show, and many other venues to spread their message of healthy living to people all over the world. They co-wrote a book called, *You, The Owner's Manual: An Insider's Guide to the Body That Will Make You Healthier and Younger*. They say that "many people equate brains with computers.... Of course, there are many differences between brains and computers, but perhaps the most important difference is that your brain doesn't automatically come with any kind of maintenance policy—especially the lifetime variety. It's up to you to provide the technical support that'll keep your hardware and software running as smoothly as possible."

Then they go on through the actual makeup of the brain and describe the following:

- **Skull**
  Because the brain has the consistency of a hard-boiled egg, it has to be protected by a skull, even at birth (at birth, the skull consists of folded plates to help get the head through the birth canal; then the plates connect and calcify [or solidify] after birth).

- **Brainstem**
  Connected to your spinal cord, it's responsible for controlling many involuntary functions, such as breathing, digestion, and heart rate.

- **Cerebellum**
  This is responsible for muscle coordination, reflexes, and balance.

- **Cerebrum**
  Much of your brain function takes place in the cerebral cortex, or outer layer of the cerebrum. It's the assembly line of human thought, where all the heavy work gets done.

- **Left Hemisphere**
  The left controls your concrete side: speech, writing, language, and calculation [mathematics].

- **Right Hemisphere**
  The right controls "your imaginative side: spatial ability, music, and intuition.

- **The Frontal Lobes**
  These control such things as planning, personality,

behavior, and emotion. The area allows us to tell right from wrong and helps us to think abstractly.

- **The Parietal Lobe**
  Most associated with touching and moving our limbs, its junction with the occipital lobe is where speech and understanding speech is located.

- **The Occipital Lobes**
  These control vision.

- **The Temporal Lobes**
  Located on both sides of your brain at about ear level, these lobes process sound and are also responsible for short-term memory.

- **Neurons**
  You have 100 billion neurons in your brain, which, if stretched out in length, would reach thirty thousand miles. That is your brain we are talking about. Each of these nerve cells contains pieces of information that need to be transmitted to another neuron so that your body can function properly. Neurons hold the information, but unless it's communicated to another neuron, it's virtually useless. That's where the edges of neurons come into play. They're called dendrites and they're like baseball catchers—they receive the pitch sent to them from other neurons. Even more important, they act like catchers by communicating to the other players on the field. Specifically, the dendrite can influence how

the signal is sent, received, and transmitted to other neurons.

- **Neurotransmitters**
These are the chemical messengers in your brain—like baseballs being tossed back and forth. When you turn a neuron on, the neurotransmitters ring or blare out to help send or receive information between neurons. When you experience neurological disorders, the cause often stems from a flaw in the neurotransmitter— if it can't transport one piece of information to another neuron, then you can't know how to complete a specific task. Also, a natural decline in the function of certain neurotransmitters is believed to make you more vulnerable to such conditions as dementia and depression.

- **Thalamus:**
Think of it as a train station in a major city that acts as a hub for many other smaller locations. That's because many different parts of the brain run through it; the thalamus takes sensory information from the spine and then fine-tunes what movements you make before they even start. It's really responsible for making actions smooth (problems with the thalamus can result in tremors, or non-smooth motor movements.)

- **Limbic system**
The limbic system isn't a structure but a series of pathways incorporating various structures

deep inside the brain, such as the hippocampus and the amygdala. Why should you care? Information gained by vision and hearing passes from the eyes and ears directly to the cortex, so we recognize the sensation and can consciously consider its meaning. On the other hand, smell sensations bypass the cortex and influence the amygdala directly, so our body responds before we can consciously process the information. The amygdala is responsible for emotions, moods, and other functions related to depression and anxiety, and the nearby hippocampus is responsible for the processing and storage of short-term memory. (Michael F. Roizen and Mehmet Oz, *You, The Owner's Manual: An Insider's Guide to the Body That Will Make You Healthier and Younger,* New York: HarperResource, 2005)

So, obviously, this is why this is very important. They go on to say that brain training is very, very possible. Neurological development is something that is a fact. "You need to understand," the two authors say, "that the brain can be retrained and it can be redesigned." But before you learn how, you need to get to know your brain a bit more.

There are four theaters of operation in the brain. Researchers say these four areas are as follows:

1. The area of perception
2. The area of attention, which includes concentration and cognition (the actual thinking process)
3. The area of basic brain and body functions like breathing

4. The area that has to do with your identity and behavior

I expect most of you have been hearing about left brain and right brain for a few years.

What does that really mean? Are you primarily a left-brain thinker or a right-brain thinker? Let's find out.

According to researchers, left-brain thinkers have eight basic characteristics:

- They are symmetrical. (Everything is balanced; things make good sense. There is an A and a B; there is a C and a D.)

- They are rational.

- They are logical.

- They are analytical.

- They are mathematical.

- They are verbal.

- They are linear. (They go from point A to point B to point C to point D in a straight line.)

- They are sequential. (They see things in an orderly fashion.)

Usually what researchers focus on is whether you are

a dominant left brain or a dominant right brain. You can be a mix of the two.

Right-brain thinkers have these characteristics:

• They are asymmetrical. (They see life in unusual and creative ways. They notice patterns that may not be observable to other people.)

• They are intuitive. (They feel connections. They sense what things mean rather than try to figure them out logically and analytically.)

• They are emotional. (They tend to navigate with feelings rather than rational thought.)

• They are holistic. (They see the bigger picture, not the analytical details.)

• They are sensitive to nonverbal communication. (They read nonverbal signals well.)

• They are visual. (They respond better to visual images than to charts and numbers.)

• They are spatial. (They can see how things and people fit together.)

• They are simultaneous, which means they see everything at once. (They are able to hold more than one thing in the mind at the same time. They can balance the whole alphabet rather than just focus on individual letters.)

Dr. Geil Browning, another brain researcher, has come up with a whole new approach to temperaments called emergenetics that is also helpful in understanding how your brain works. She believes you have a genetic tendency to be a certain temperament type, and your brain enforces that because you inherited certain tendencies. But as you live your life, other experiences will emerge that interact with and can even change your tendencies. She calls this emergenetics. As they emerge, your actual personality is formed in the emerging of life experiences and your genetic components. Dr. Browning says that in her research, she has found four types (or some combination) of people:

1. Analytical people are the logical, rational ones.

2. Structural people are the ones who walk into a room and rearrange the furniture and line up the books. They want every detail to be right; they can only work well when there is clearly an organized structure. These people are very methodical.

3. Conceptual people are the visionaries, the artistic, imaginative ones. They see all the connections; they are definitely right-brain people.

4. Social people are people-oriented people. They relate through people, by people, about people, and for people. (A good example of the social person is a woman I met who went to a monastery for two days of solitude. During those two days, she did not speak to anyone because the whole purpose was to

worship God and reflect on her relationship with Him. It was hard to discipline herself to do this—but she did—and she had a great time. When she got home, she spent the first eight to nine hours calling everybody she knew to tell them how great it was to have a time of solitude. She was so social she was bursting to relate her experience with as many friends as possible.)

The important thing for you to do now is to understand who you are. Are you a person who is more left brain or more right brain? Are you more social or more analytical? Once you understand your personality, your tendencies, and your temperament, you can better train your brain to assist you in developing the life you want.

Now, let me tell you about another part of the brain I believe is exciting. I am talking about the concept of plasticity, which is an understanding of the flexibility of the brain and its ability to create new growth, new neural pathways. Plasticity is the term used by brain researchers and neurologists to mean the moldability, or changeability, of the human brain. What they have found is that new neural pathways can be created. If you make the right decisions, and if you make those decisions long enough (you stick to them), you will create new neural pathways. You will form chemical and electrical responses in your brain that have never existed before.

In 1986, Dr. David Snowdon, now retired from the University of Kentucky, conducted a research project on a group of Roman Catholic nuns that illustrates plasticity in an effective way. The Nun Study (as it was called) followed the lives of members of the School Sisters of Notre Dame in Mankato, Minnesota. Dr. Snowdon studied these women and discovered several things: They were healthy (they grew their own food and exercised); they were happy because they loved God and helped people; they had great social relationships, a great community (they spent time with each other and loved one another).

He also found they used what he called massive intellectual stimulation. He said they created new neural pathways well into their 90s. The nuns agreed to have their brains autopsied after they died, which showed they had the brains of younger women—all because of massive intellectual stimulation. A group of the nuns, while in their 80s, decided to read nineteenth century Russian literature. They wanted to experience the literature directly, so they learned to read Russian. Dr. Snowdon said these nuns were always doing mental activities such as that. They were always stimulating and challenging and stretching their minds, and their brains responded; they became younger. Almost every month, their brains created new neural pathways, new neurological responses, based on the stimulation the nuns were giving them.

A similar study that is often quoted when discussing brain plasticity is one involving London taxi drivers. I love London. It is a favorite city I have visited almost one hundred times. The cab drivers of London are outstanding, the best in the world. But to become licensed drivers, they must pass a very difficult test (known as the Knowledge), which takes years of study.

The cabbies-to-be have to learn detailed information on everything about this city, including some 25,000 streets within a six-mile radius from Charing Cross (my favorite part of this city). The London cab drivers must know all of them—where they start, where they finish, and where they cross—to pass this test. They also need to know any places that might interest a rider: restaurants, hospitals, schools, churches, and more. Every cab driver is required to have this knowledge.

Some time ago, a study was done of the brains of these cab drivers. The researchers, Eleanor Maguire and Katherine Woollett of University College London, discovered the cabbies all had larger medial temporal lobes. The posterior hippocampus, the area of the brain important for memory, was bigger than normal—and continued growing as the cabbies progressed through the Knowledge. That part of their brain got bigger because they were doing what Dr. Snowdon called massive intellectual stimulation.

That is what I mean by plasticity. You can alter your brain; you can help it get younger (get better) by massive intellectual stimulation. So if you want a brain breakthrough, you must change your brain. And you do that by what you bring into your brain, by what stimulation you allow into your brain, which I will discuss later.

Plasticity is a huge concept because it gives you hope: It is possible to change, to redirect your brain. It is possible to create new neural pathways. You may find something very hard to do; but if you can think the right thoughts, do the right things, and follow the right pattern, you can create a new neural pathway. (Research at the David Geffen School of Medicine at UCLA (DGSOM) estimates it takes about thirty-two days to do this.)

Once those new paths are formed, it will be easier to think those good thoughts and perform those good habits. Plasticity is everything. It means that you are not stuck. If you will just get serious about reprogramming, redirecting, restructuring, and redoing your neural pathways, you will change any harmful patterns. Now, I am not saying that will change you spiritually. I believe only God can do that, but this can have a radical effect on your life.

Think of it like this: Change your brain, and you will change your performance. Change your performance, and you will change your results.

Chapter 2

The Care and Feeding

God has given you a gift. The power and potential of your brain is amazing: you can be more than you have ever been, and you can accomplish more than you have ever accomplished. The future is bright and hopeful—but only if you take care of your brain.

Will you allow me a play on words to illustrate what I mean? *Train Your Brain for Success* is the title of this book. But what if I were to reverse the order of the words? It would sound something like this: Your brain is like a train. Seems a bit over the top, doesn't it?

Actually, that little play on words is a true statement: your brain is like a train. It is the engine of your physical life, of your biological existence. Your brain pulls the cars of your life (family, entertainment, social contacts, children, finances, mind, imagination, and your relationship with God), just as the locomotive pulls the cars of a train. And just as a train needs diesel to run, so your brain needs fuel (how you nurture your mind, both physically and mentally) to function properly. To make sure your brain is prepared for success, to make certain you are ready for the adventure of a lifetime, you must nourish it. You need a healthy brain, which means you must focus on its care and feeding. You must do something for your brain so it can do wonderful things for you. So, what can you do to take care of your brain?

That is simple:

1. Eat protein.

Protein is the building block of life. It is the building block of cellular activity, and your brain is filled with cells. The brain requires protein; it needs a steady supply of it. Yes, you need vitamins, minerals, and other nutrients; but your brain thrives on protein. So if you want a healthy, youthful, energized brain, you have to start with protein; and the only way to get enough protein is by eating it. You need to get it from your diet. You need to eat protein-rich foods, which help with brain development and brain energy.

2. Avoid chronic stress.

Some stress is harmless, part of the ins and outs of life, part of maneuvering through human existence. Some stress happens because there is a moment of response, and then it is over. You are walking down the sidewalk, and you hear a booming sound behind you. You do not know the source of the sound, but the sudden noise and the effect on your senses create a response: a startle reflex, a moment of stress. Adrenaline, cortisol, and other hormones surge through your system. But when you perceive there is no danger (the boom is not repeated or nothing happens), you calm down and continue with your walk. Yes, it is stress. But it is not chronic stress; it comes and it goes. You have a moment of stressful response, and then it is over.

Chronic stress is different. It is ongoing, unresolved stress that gradually wears you down and weakens you. (Chronic comes from the Greek word *chronos*, meaning time.) Chronic stress is stress that continues over time. The stress you are experiencing never goes away, so your immune system is weakened. There is a continual drain on your cellular resources, and you find you are not as energetic as you were. You become distracted, sometimes mentally confused. You are tired more often, and you may have difficulty sleeping, all because of this underlying current of unresolved chronic stress.

What does chronic stress do to the brain? The chemical that is released when you experience stress is cortisol, which is actually a hormone. Cortisol is good for you when you only experience it temporarily, like walking on the sidewalk and hearing a loud noise. Cortisol gets you ready to fight or flee—to defend yourself or run for cover. But cortisol is not intended to be continually in your system. When it is regularly being produced, the cellular walls in your brain are challenged, and you end up weak and worn down. Your body becomes confused because you are experiencing constant secretions of a chemical you are only supposed to experience on particular moments.

Dr. Daniel Amen, a well-known physician, psychiatrist, and best-selling author, has two terms he uses in relation to stress: Important But Manageable events (IBM) and Nagging Unfinished Tasks (NUTs). The IBM events are important, so there is a little stress, a little concern involved. These events may involve some preparation and anxiety, but they are momentary. They come and they go. The NUTs make up a big part of your chronic stress. They bring a nagging sense that something is not complete: I have so many responsibilities hanging onto me; I don't know how to handle them all. I don't know how to finish them. There is no closure. And if your Nagging Unfinished Tasks accumulate, or if more are added to your life, your stress levels get worse. You go through each day carrying a heavy load of chronic nervous tension. You become affected biochemically, attitudinally and emotionally.

Chronic stress is your enemy: It suppresses your immune system and challenges your sense of well-being and confidence. It is detrimental to the performance and health of your brain. Get rid of it. I believe this is one area where God can help. Over 300 times in the Bible He says, "Fear not." He is continually offering His grace, power, comfort, support, and help so you do not live life afraid. God wants to lower your stress by encouraging you to trust in Him. So, chronic stress is bad for the brain, and it hinders your ability to perform well.

3. Experience new things.
The brain thrives on newness; it loves being challenged. Your brain will create new neural

pathways based on your willingness to experience new things in new ways, on your willingness to receive new information.

Dr. Peter Drucker, the famous management consultant, died at the age of ninety-six after playing a round of golf in Palm Springs, California. He was active, energetic, focused, effective, and creative right until the end. When he was fifty years old, he made a decision: every two years, he would learn something new. And he followed that program for the rest of his life. It kept his brain young and healthy. When he died, he was studying the sewer systems of medieval Paris. That may sound boring to you, but he found it fascinating. He was learning information he never knew existed, and he was excited about how his brain was responding.

You need new experiences. I talked to a man who told me he challenges his brain every week by going home a different way. He lives in a medium-sized city, so he can only do that so long; but for now, that is how he is training his mind. "I go home on a route I've never taken. I see images of the city I've not noticed before. I learn something new, which stretches my brain and excites my emotions," he told me.

So, have new experiences. Learn new information; read new books. Watch movies you do not normally watch. Go to places you rarely go; talk to people you barely know. All of those situations challenge, train, and feed your brain. You are causing your mind to have chemical and electrical responses, which then create new neural pathways that make it younger. So open yourself to new ways of interacting with life and let your brain develop and increase its power.

4. Sharpen your memory.

Memory is a great part of brain health and vitality. Practice learning and practice remembering. Some of this is simply a matter of repetition. You remember your phone number because you repeat it frequently. You remember certain pieces of information because you use them every day. Repetition is the secret to memory. If you focus on something long enough, you will remember it. Practice memory; practice learning how to improve your memory, and you will feed your brain.

5. Listen to music.

Your brain responds well to symmetry, harmony, and rhythm. It responds to music that feels complete and has a positive image. If you listen to music that is depressing and jarring, your brain will react negatively. If you listen to music that makes you nervous, your brain will cause you to feel anxious. When you tap your foot (or finger) to a musical beat, something just feels right because your brain is in its comfort zone. It is responding to a sense of organization, a connection, an up and down that seems right. (And if you cannot keep time with music, practice. Sit down, pay attention to the beat, and practice tapping your foot or finger. You may never become great, but you will improve— and your brain will thank you.) So listen to music. Your brain is fed by the harmonies, the balance, the musical notes, the positive impact, and the rhythm.

6. Focus on smell.

Of the five senses, smell is the one that is instantly processed by the brain. Certain smells can cause an immediate reaction. If you smell something bad, you are disgusted by the odor. If you smell something good, you are attracted to it. Dr. Amen talks about how smell can relax and refresh your brain. Scents such as vanilla and lavender can create a sense of calmness; they help you think clearly and feel happy.

7. Get your blood flowing.

There is one more physical ingredient involved in the care and feeding of your brain, and that is blood flow. Your brain needs oxygen; it cannot breathe on its own. It gets its oxygen from your blood, which flows best when you engage in aerobic activities. When you exercise, you increase the action of your circulatory system. Blood is pumped through your body, carrying the oxygen you are breathing in. Your brain needs to be oxygenated by blood flow. And when that blood flows through your brain, it loves you because its health and vitality are increasing. The possibilities for your success increase because of something as simple and basic as blood flow.

If you are uncertain of your physical abilities, check with a doctor first. Have a good physical examination. You may not have exercised regularly at this point in your life, so begin by taking a walk. I have been running since 1992. I have had over twenty years of regular physical exercise, jogging around forty miles a week. Sure, it has become a habit; but I also love it. I love how I feel: I sleep well. My blood pressure is nearly perfect. I have a sitting pulse rate that is low. I am happy after I run (a feeling that lasts all day). Running is a very special time for me. As I move, I pray in my spirit; I use the time to communicate with my heavenly Father.

So, I encourage you to exercise, even if it is just taking a simple walk around the block. You will release endorphins (feel-good chemicals) that not only will help your health but also will give you an opportunity to build your brain.

Dr. Roizen and Dr. Oz, in their book I referenced earlier, speak about simple ways to test your brain health. This is an easy test you can do to determine your level of brain flexibility and health: Stand with your feet flat on the floor, posture erect—back straight, shoulders back—then close your eyes and lift one foot. (It does not matter which one.) See if you can balance on one foot with your eyes closed. The longer you can stand without losing your equilibrium, the better. (For those of you forty-five and over, fifteen seconds is very good.)

If you can do that, your brain is receiving adequate blood flow. It is compensating for the lack of sight and working to keep you balanced. If you topple over, you need to work on some of these areas. You might need to relax your brain, eat more protein, experience more new things, or work more crossword puzzles. If your brain cannot compensate for a lack of vision to enable you to balance yourself, then you need to think about helping your brain get younger, more flexible, and more energetic. (I am not giving medical advice here. I borrowed this simple test from their book to encourage you to check your balance and your brain's ability to function even when your eyes are closed. Do not read too much into this if it does not work for you.)

The two brain researchers I mentioned earlier, Gillian Butler and Tony Hope, have what they call the seven signs of good mind management, which I believe are connected to the care and feeding of your brain. I have borrowed their list and added one of my own at the end.

1. Manage your time.

Butler and Hope say that managing yourself and your time is a sign of good mind management. There is only so much time in your day. So when you learn to arrange your day and manage your responsibilities, you are mentally healthy. If you find you are not getting enough sleep (because you are doing things at the end of the day that you should have done at the beginning), then you are not taking charge of your schedule. Experiencing continual organizational breakdowns is mismanagement. A sign of good mind management is when you can organize your life reasonably well. You may never be a genius at bringing order, but you should do a good enough job that you have a tolerably calm, balanced life. So, manage yourself, your schedule, and your time effectively.

2. Face your problems.

You need to look your difficulty in the eye and recognize it for what it is. You need to accept reality, then look for a solution. If you avoid your problems, they get worse, or you never develop the skills you need to handle life effectively.

My mentor, Dr. David Seamands, a tremendous counselor respected all over the United States, said, in his opinion, the first rule of good counseling was to help people face reality—whatever it was. He told about a young woman who lived in a nearby city who came to him for help. She had been a tennis player with a possibility of playing professionally. She had injured her foot and needed to have surgery. The surgeon who operated on her was drunk and botched the operation, ruining her foot. It was a tragedy for her young life. She was getting married soon, so this bitter, angry young woman came to Dr. Seamands for help. She blamed the doctor. She blamed God. She blamed everybody. Dr. Seamands listened to her griping and blaming for half an hour. Finally, he looked at her and said, "Your foot will not get better."

She stood up, "How dare you!"

He said, "It will not get better. What are you going to do about it?"

She stomped out of the office. About two or three weeks later, she called and asked for an appointment. She was still angry, but she came in and asked, "Dr. Seamands, what did you mean by that?"

He said, "I mean this: You will never put your life back

together; you will never find God's plan for you if you swim in this sea of bitterness. If you continue to wallow in defeatism and victimhood, your life is finished."

He went on, "You will not play tennis professionally; your foot cannot bear your weight any longer. You will always have a limp unless some new surgical technique or technology comes along. You will experience this difficulty the rest of your life—that is your reality. And until you face your reality, you will never be able to do anything about it."

Gradually, she accepted his counsel. She became a beautiful Christian, with a wonderful marriage and family. She came back to Dr. Seamunds to admit that she was having a happy life experiencing God's guidance. She still liked tennis, but she had found so many other things to do. She was a contented woman, and it all started with facing her problem.

3. Develop problem-solving skills.
This is the logical next step. First, you face your problem, then you develop a plan to do something about it. You face your difficulty, and you organize a plan to attack it. You face your complication, and then you solve your dilemma as much as it can be solved.

4. Treat yourself well.
This does not mean be lazy, give up, and become a bum. Taking care of yourself means you must eat well, exercise regularly, get a good night's sleep, and take a break when you need one. When you take care of

yourself, your brain responds by not being in constant hyperdrive. Learn to look after yourself.

5. Learn the art of relaxing your brain.

This is similar to treating yourself well, but Butler and Hope make it a separate point, which is a good idea because sometimes you need to turn off your brain. There are times when you need to stop all the thinking, all the processing, all the worrying. You need to shut down and do something that is completely relaxing. When I travel on an airplane, I take a book that is easy to read, maybe science fiction or fantasy. (My good friend Dr. Mark Barrett calls it brain candy.) Well, it may be brain candy, but it is relaxing to my mind. Sometimes you need to do something like that. You need to shut down and let your brain recover.

6. Choose your perspective.

Perspective has to do with how you view something. I live in a small town in southeastern Kentucky, a beautiful place on the Cumberland Plateau of the Appalachian Mountains. There are trees everywhere. We have big trees all over town, including the street where I live.

I came home from a trip two weeks ago and noticed that one of the big elm trees was gone. When I inquired about it, I was told that a disease had rotted the inside, and so it had to be cut down. I was very disappointed, but understood that the tree's time had come.

Well, this week I came home and found another big, wonderful tree gone. I was told that this elm was cut down because the city was erecting new power poles, and it was in the way. My street is now without two of its most beautiful trees, which were across the street from one another.

I was walking out of my yard last night, and I saw one of my neighbors. After greeting him, I crossed over to his house and said, "We will have to plant some new trees on our street; we are losing them."

"You know," he said, "I noticed they were gone. My immediate thought was, 'We will have so much wonderful sunshine on our street'."

As I headed back to my house, I said to myself, "He's got a great attitude." It reminded me of the positive pencils my daughter used to sell. The most popular one said, "Attitude is everything" —which is a prime ingredient of perspective. My neighbor chose to see our partially treeless street as a place of abundant sunshine. How you look (positively or negatively) at something, how you choose to see a situation is what makes life a happy one.

Your thoughts are critical in this process. Dr. Daniel Amen talks about the thought sequence, something I speak of frequently in different seminars. Your thought sequence is simple: You have a thought, and the moment you have a thought, a chemical is released in your brain. The moment that chemical is released, an electrical charge is generated. When an electrical charge is generated, you have an emotion that matches your original thought, and a new neural pathway is begun—all because you thought a thought.

And you go through this process whether the thought is a positive or a negative one. There is a difference though. Although the negative thought creates the same sequence of reactions, the result is a negative result, which affects your brain and neural pathways. You started a negative path when you could have started a positive one. So make sure all your mental pathways are positive pathways.

7. Build your self-confidence and self-esteem.
If you feel good about yourself, if you have confidence in your abilities, if you believe in what you do and in what you can accomplish, you will feed your brain. Self-assurance and a positive self-esteem nourish the brain.

8. Spend time praying.
This is the one I am adding because I believe your life is better managed when you depend on God. He has a wonderful purpose for you, an exciting future. God has a design for your life, and when you experience it, your life is better. He loves you.

Chapter 3

The Tracks

In the previous chapter, you learned the brain was like a train with an engine and cars. The engine is your brain, and the cars represent your life (job, family, church, friends). You learned that just as a train needs diesel to run so your brain also needs fuel. Oxygen, water, and food are gas for your engine; things you read, watch, or talk about are also nourishment going into your brain.

Now, to carry that analogy further, I will say that just as a real train runs on tracks, so your brain pulls you in a certain direction. The tracks represent how you think; they represent your thoughts. I assumed I was a big believer in positive attitude and positive thinking, but I learned things in my research I never knew about positive thinking.

"Wait a minute, Ron," you say. "I've heard all this stuff about positive thinking before. I know I'm supposed to think positively." But brain training is more than a positive attitude. It is a way to expand your abilities, increase your intelligent response to life, and help you elevate your strengths.

As I said, tracks are your thoughts, which determine everything: where you go, how you go, and what you will do. How you think is absolutely critical to where you go.

For example, a railroad engineer has his locomotive fueled properly; he has all the cars attached and ready to go. But if he follows tracks that lead over a cliff, what good is his engine? What good is the fuel? Tracks that lead over a cliff will cause a disaster. Tracks that do not lead anywhere will dead-end. If your engine is headed toward a dead end, it will simply stop because the tracks go no further, which is why your thinking really matters. You want to get your brain-train on a positive series of tracks.

So the question is, are you running on positive tracks or negative tracks? Let's find out. There are eight negative tracks you want to exit, and eight positive ones you want to get onto. Let's look at the negative ones first.

1. You need to get off the negative brain track of allowance.

Psychologists talk about what they call rumination (going over something again and again and again). This track is the mental decision to allow certain negative elements to stay in your mind. You allow yourself to dwell on past errors in judgment. You allow yourself to focus on past relationship disasters. You allow yourself to remember negatives you should forget. (Yes, you need to learn from your mistakes, which is vital to your success; but do not dwell on them.) Cows chew their cud; you ruminate. Something happens, and you will not let it go. You keep chewing on it; you keep thinking about it. The rumination wears you out and drains your energy. The negative track of allowance is when you allow yourself to keep thinking about your past failures and disappointments. You are permitting—and it is a choice—into your mind those negatives that keep you on the wrong track.

2. You need to get off the negative brain track of blame lock.

This is when you get locked into certain negative patterns. Dr. Jeffrey Schwartz of the David Geffen School of Medicine at UCLA is an international expert on the treatment of obsessive-compulsive behaviors. He believes that obsessive-compulsive behaviors are hard to change because they are connected to neural pathways (biochemical pathways) that have been developed over the years in a person's brain. He believes that the best way to change wrong-behavior practices is to replace them with good-behavior practices.

For example, if you want to break a bad habit, you replace it with a good habit. Dr. Schwartz says these repetitive patterns can actually change the wiring of your brain, but it takes time. If you want to replace a bad pattern with a new pattern (to create a new neurological pathway), he says it will take forty-one days of practicing the new activity to create the new pathway. It will take forty-one days to give your brain the chemical, neurological, and electrical support it will need to build and keep the new pattern.

3. You need to get off the negative brain track of categories.

You devise categories in your brain that ensnare you. For example, if you tell yourself, "I am a clumsy person," you create a mental classification into which you place yourself. You trap yourself inside that category; you pigeonhole yourself. And because you have created a "Department of Clumsiness" in your mind, you think you are clumsy and will probably act it.

When you think thoughts such as I'm a weak person; I can never lose weight; I'm bad with money; or I'm no good with relationships, you create a negative domain. You think you fit the category, but, really, you created it and the neurological pathways to support that category. And so you get on a wrong brain track.

But you do not have to stay on it. Let me give you a little exercise to help you get off this track. Many of you ask "Can I..." questions: "Can I do something?" "Can I build this business?" "Can I succeed in this marriage?" "Can I improve my walk with God?" "Can I lose weight?" "Can I manage my money better?" "Can I get out of debt?" Asking the "Can I..." questions keeps you in a category because it introduces doubt.

Instead, add the word "How" to your questions: "How

can I do something?" "How can I build this business?" "How can I succeed in this marriage?" "How can I improve my walk with God?" "How can I lose weight?" "How can I manage my money better?" "How can I get out of debt?" When you do the mental health process that I wrote about in the previous chapter, you become a problem solver. You think things through; your mind clears, and you figure things out. So if you change that one phrase from "Can I do it?" to "How can I do it?" you will get off this negative brain track.

4. You need to get off the negative brain track of context.

The previous point is about putting yourself in a category, but context is about what surrounds you. Your context makes sense of your life. If you see yourself in a situation thinking, "This will never change," all you have done is surrounded yourself with negative context. You have created a negative environment: "These are my circumstances; there is nothing I can do about them. This is my life; I can't change it." You have trapped yourself in that context, and you have to make the choice to get yourself out.

Context has to do with who you are. For example, you see a gathering of successful people (the context of them is who they are together as a group), but you do not see yourself in that group. Do you know what will happen? If you do not see yourself as an accomplished, welcomed member of that group, you will pull away from them and not become part of that successful crowd of people. They have not rejected you; they have not pushed you out or refused to let you in. You have done this to yourself. You decided you did not belong in their group, in that success context. You could not see yourself in the company of these notable people, so you withdrew. This is why the whole idea of context is so psychologically important.

5. You need to get off the negative brain track of emotional tagging.

You put a physical tag (or label) on something to identify it. You can also attach an emotion to certain things. Growing up, some of you may have fastened an emotional tag to money (for example, guilt or the fear of materialism). Whether you did the tagging, or someone else did the tagging and you absorbed it, you have tagged money. You have attached a label; you have connected emotions (which may not be rational) to money. So, whenever the opportunity to make money presents itself, your brain brings up the tag and emotions come pouring out. (You can also tag things in a positive way. You can look at your money and say, "Hey, there's nothing wrong with money. It has been honestly earned, and I am generous. My life is blessed because I bring home my paycheck. That's a good thing.")

I met a young man after I spoke at a university where I had asked, "What can you do to succeed more in life?" After the lecture, the young student slowly made his way across the room and said, "I'm a junior, and I major in communications. I can't seem to get a focus on my life." I talked to him for a while and soon realized this young man lacked restraint; he was disorganized and lazy. But when I mentioned the word discipline to him, he immediately backed away from me. Somehow, he had emotionally tagged self-discipline. He thought that if he restrained himself, he could not love life; he could not be spontaneous or free. In his mind, discipline was some form of slavery, and he wanted nothing to do with it—which was why his life was falling apart academically and professionally. He had tagged work and self-control with a negative emotion. So the moment he recognized any need to be disciplined, or whenever anyone pointed out the need for him to be disciplined, that emotional tag surfaced. His brain chemistry kicked in, and the negative emotions flowed—all because of the emotional tagging.

Your emotional tags can be changed, but it is not easy to do. Dr. Jeffrey Schwartz writes about rerouting, or re-creating, new circuitry in your brain by repetitive positive responses. He says that when you have had so much negative repetitive response, you will need positive repetitive response to retrain your brain and create new neurological pathways that can replace your old negative responses with the new positive ones.

6. You need to get off the negative brain track of mental fog.

The word fog creates an immediate picture in my mind: the heavy, thick mist on the streets of London in the old Sherlock Holmes books and movies. There is a mental fog created in your brain circuitry when you continually start things and do not finish them. It is called the fog of incompletion. If you are a person who starts something but never finishes it, your circuitry will become one of incompletion. So whenever you do want to finish something, your brain will become your own worst enemy because you have allowed yourself to be in this pattern for so long.

That is one danger of setting a new goal and giving up too quickly. If you create this mental fog of incompletion, your brain circuitry will respond, making it harder and harder for you to follow through—which is why it is so vital to teach children to finish their tasks. When children are taught to carry out their responsibilities without excuses, their training will imprint on their growing, flexible brains, making it far easier for them to be responsible adults who keep their commitments.

If you did not receive this imprinting as a child, you may have to retrain your brain. You will need to invest the time and effort to create new pathways, but once you do, your brain will become your biggest supporter, your greatest helper. It will then become easier and easier to make and keep commitments.

Athletes develop muscle memory through dedicated practice. They also develop circuitry memory that helps them train in a particular way so that when they compete, their brain (their training, imprinting, circuitry memory) is their biggest ally. In the same way, you can create new neurological memory that can cause your brain to supply the support you need to move forward.

7. You need to get off the negative brain track of predetermined definitions.
A predetermined definition means you have already

defined something in your mind, and you do not think you need to examine it again. (This is similar to being prejudiced against people when you do not know them.)

This negative brain track is a characterization of who you are, an established definition of what you are like. If you think you are good or not good at something, you have already determined a definition that traps you. You have chosen a mental description, and your brain will cooperate with the definition of yourself that you created in your mind—which will form new neurological pathways.

That is what is so fascinating about this: You will form new brain circuitry that will actually make your definition seem real to you, even when it is wrong. (Maybe you will never be as good as somebody who is a natural in a particular area, but you could improve. Yet many times you will not even try, because your brain has been trained to communicate your determination of yourself.)

If your mind operates on the basis of predetermined definitions, then you will always shut the door on your own possibilities. You may miss what could be a phenomenal opportunity for you because you are depending on old brain circuitry. (A sign you are allowing your old predetermined definitions to control you is the way you talk to yourself: "Well, we have always done it this way"; or "You know what? We do need to do that, but it has never worked; so I don't think it will work for our company." Those are old ways of thinking.) Your brain acts old because you are using predetermined definitions that have created an old brain.

So, what do you do? You need new brain chemistry. When you train your brain to welcome new opportunities, you make your brain more youthful, which is what you want. A youthful brain starts by eliminating predetermined definitions.

8. You need to get off the negative brain track of future projections.

When your future predictions are full of doubt and fear, you are on a negative track.

Dr. Ellen Langer, a professor in the Psychology Department at Harvard University, has written about the psychological aspects of worry that apply to brain training. She did a study on worry (which she calls projecting your current fears into your future) to determine the mental state people are in when they worry.

Dr. Langer found that 90 percent of people's worries usually fall into three areas: unimportant, unlikely, and unresolved. The unimportant area encompasses those things that will not matter if the fearful thing happens. For example, you are giving a presentation in six months, and you fear if you do not lose five pounds, you will not look as good. The five pounds will not matter much (i.e. they are unimportant) as long as you wear something appropriate and do a good job with the presentation. The unlikely area encompasses those worries that are probably not going to happen. And the unresolved area contains those things that will not change, no matter how much fear you have; so you are wasting your time and mental energy by worrying. Some things cannot be resolved; they must be accepted as they are.

Dr. Langer's patients were sometimes so ripped apart and dominated by fear and worry she had to come up with some approaches that would rescue them from their faulty thinking. She devised seven techniques for the elimination of worry:

1. The One-Hundred-Year Rule

Dr. Langer says she borrowed this one from Winston Churchill, who would say, "In a hundred years, will this thing I'm worried about really matter?" When he used his one-hundred-year rule, he could eliminate many things he feared.

2. The Mental Calculator

Dr. Langer suggests using the mental-calculator rule: Is all the worry and fear worth it? Calculate how much your anxiety is worth. Ask yourself: "Is the stress, the distraction worth it? Is the diversion of my energy into the fearful projection of the future worth it? Is it worth the way it divides my mind? The way it spoils my emotions? The way it distracts me from my focus, my energy, my family?"

3. The Measuring Rod

This technique, she says, is where you ask yourself, "How bad can things really be? If such and such happens, how bad will it be? Is it survivable? Can I get out of it? Can I get through it?"

4. The Action Transfer

She recommends taking that mental energy and transferring it into action. When you do something about your fear, the power of that fear shrinks. You transfer your energy from worry to constructive action.

5. The Crowded-out Approach

She says if you are busy enough, you can displace, or force out, your fear. Winston Churchill often struggled with depression. Numerous historians say Churchill overcame his bouts of depression by staying busy. He "crowded out" his fears with busyness.

6. The Mental Box

With this technique, she suggests imagining a box and putting your fear into that box. Once your fear is placed inside, she says to mentally place a lid and then take a key to mentally lock it. As you put the box away, say to yourself, "Here are my worry and my fear. I know where they are. I know where to find them. I'll just leave them in the box." When you do this, Dr. Langer says, you often simply forget about your anxiety.

7. The Brick Wall

Dr. Langer advises mentally constructing a brick wall between you and the fear. You leave the fear on the other side of the wall, and you go on with your life. You know it is there. You know you can always break through the wall and get to it, but you move on.

I hope you are getting a good picture of how your brain works and how your thinking affects its chemistry. If you are on a negative train track, you will not go where you want to go; if your thinking is pessimistic, your life will go in the wrong direction. But the brain can be retrained, which is the whole idea of plasticity (the flexible nature of the brain). It is not locked into some way that cannot ever be changed. Isn't that exciting? So, remove yourself from the negative tracks and get ready to train your brain to travel on positive ones.

There are ways to train your brain in a positive way. If the negative tracks can pull you back that dramatically, can you imagine what the positive tracks can do? This is exciting stuff. Here are the eight positive brain train tracks based on the latest research:

1. The Mental Filter

Dr. Daniel Amen uses an imaging technique known as SPECT (Single Photon Emission Computed Tomography), which measures blood flow to the body's tissues and organs, to determine how thoughts affect blood flow to different areas of the brain. Dr. Amen says positive and negative thoughts release chemicals that affect the deep limbic part of the brain. Through the use of SPECT scans, he found that happy, positive thoughts cool down the deep limbic system of the brain, where emotion and feelings of motivation originate. He says thoughts that are critical, harmful, or harsh are like biological pollution and affect every cell in the body.

You may be committed to positive thinking; but if you

still allow detrimental thoughts, you may actually be harming yourself by heating your deep limbic system, which will then overflow with negative emotion. However, the chemical reactions that occur when you cool down your deep limbic system with happy, positive thoughts, according to Dr. Amen's research, will have you feeling better. You will be more motivated, more focused, happier. This is your brain rewiring itself to help you.

Do you remember the thought sequence I referenced earlier? I said Dr. Amen explained it this way:

- You have a thought, whether positive or negative.

- A chemical that is coded by that thought is released.

- The chemical triggers an electrical charge.

- The charge creates an emotion based on the original thought.

Well, this thought sequence shows why the mental filter is so important. All the reactions just described start with your thought, so it is essential you train yourself to think positive ones.

2. The Listening Brain

Your brain's chemistry is affected by words, not just the ones you think, but ones you say. Your brain reacts immediately to a spoken word.

In his book *Predictably Irrational: The Hidden Forces*

That Shape Our Decisions, author Dan Ariely writes about the talking brain. He mentions a study where students were asked to verbalize words they were reading. Hidden within the paragraph they were told to read aloud were words that suggested an elderly individual: old, decrepit, ancient. The students were then asked to walk down a hallway to turn their paper in to another professor. Almost all the students who read the paragraph out loud walked like an old person: they shuffled along with their heads down and seemed almost feeble. The researchers then arranged for another test group to read a different paragraph, which also had inserted words that were not directly related to the content. These students read the paragraph and, according to the research in this book, walked down the hallway with a spring in their steps. They were lively, more dynamic. Interestingly, the students did not seem to recognize why they responded as they did. Their brains had reacted to the words and had created a physical response in them.

Dr. Ariely also carried out a study on cheating with two more groups of students. Before taking a test, one group was asked to list ten books off their high school reading list, and the other group was asked to recall the Ten Commandments. He found that even if they did not believe in the Bible, the second group's attitudes toward cheating changed. Those who wrote out the Ten Commandments expressed an aversion to cheating. Even when given opportunities to cheat, none did. However, many students in the other test group, without knowing they were being observed, cheated.

This researcher is saying that your brain is greatly affected by the words you use. Think before you use obscene language, before you use words that are ugly and coarse, uncivilized and unrefined. I know movies use profanity, and society often considers swearing cool. But foul language affects your brain; it affects your attitude toward other people. (There are preliminary indications suggesting that aggressiveness in someone may be affected by the language he uses taken from other people and situations.) So make sure that when you talk out loud, you are reinforcing the right brain chemistry for your success.

3. The Aware Person (Mindfulness)

This is the power of personal observation, the development of a keen self-awareness. You need to observe yourself honestly by asking the questions, "Why am I getting these results? What is the truth about me? my performance? my behavior?" The more mindful you become, the more insights you will gain. Your brain will cooperate, and your circuitry will become your ally.

Mindfulness will allow you to evaluate your actions. It will give you a better understanding of why that person did not buy into your business, or why you did not get that promotion. Learn to calm your mind and quiet your actions. I am not telling you to be overly introspective and inwardly focused, but you need to examine your behavior: Why did I react (or behave) like that? Why did I yell at my husband? Why did I scream at my kids? Why did I get mad at my wife? Why did I get excited about that meeting? Why did I lie when somebody invited me to an event I didn't want to attend? Why did I do what I just did? Analyze yourself; break down the components of your behavior and develop mindfulness. Let your mind flow into the depths of your thinking to reveal why you do what you do.

4. The Association Flow

Dr. Jeff Brown, Assistant Clinical Professor in the Department of Psychiatry at Harvard Medical School, has uncovered some important insights, which I have included as positive tracks four, five, and six.

Dr. Brown says your energy flow is affected by whether you associate your behavior with a hero. (He is a sport psychologist, so many of his examples come from the world of competitive sports.) Dr. Brown writes that if you mentally picture someone you admire (focusing on how he does things, how he responds, how he operates), you can create a hero response in your brain circuitry so that whenever you imagine that someone, there will be what he calls "a positive association flow." Your idol will inspire you, and the hero imprint will give you energy. The association flow will enhance your ability to perform.

He warns, though, that you have to attach yourself to the right role models and the right performances (actions) for the right reasons. If you want to be a good public speaker and improve your communication skills, then you should identify someone who is already a good public speaker, so that when you get up in front of people, you can imagine that person standing with you, encouraging you. Brown says that is how the mental process works. You imagine your hero telling you that you can do it. If you are fearful, you picture a person with courage and imagine yourself following the example of a courageous person, which, according to Dr. Brown, creates a positive association flow and helps you become more like the person you admire.

5. The Pre-Competition Routine
Dr. Brown has taught many Olympic-level athletes to use this technique because it makes them feel like winners before they ever compete.

Billy Graham, one of my heroes, said that for years, before speaking to thousands of people about a personal relationship with Jesus Christ, he went through his own pre-competition routine: He would rest in the afternoon; eat a sandwich around six o'clock and then take a hot bath. He said the hot bath would relax him and help him feel great for speaking.

So for your own routine, determine what calms you, what makes you feel like a winner before a presentation. Identify those few things that make you feel at your best and create your own pre-competition routine.

6. The Perfect Picture (Visualization)
Dr. Brown writes about being picture perfect, which is the classic idea of visualization. The baseball player who envisions hitting the ball and knocking it over the left-field fence and the golfer who imagines the putt going into the hole are both using this technique. It

really does work. If you visualize enough, you can actually create a picture-perfect response. Your brain coordinates the muscles as you mentally picture the action you want to complete. You cannot create that response by suddenly deciding to do this. You have to train yourself by visualizing it over and over in your mind.

7. The Mental Script

Research has found that mental stories are constantly running in your mind. Your brain chemistry and electro-neurological circuits backup those stories. You have created the story of your life, and your brain is always looking for ways to confirm that story.

Let me give you an example: B.J. was a happy, outgoing guy who never had a problem. He was almost thirty years old when he suddenly lost his job because the company downsized. As a newly hired manager, he was one of the first ones to be dismissed. B.J. took it hard. He became depressed, which affected his family and his health, because losing his job did not fit his mind script. The movie in his mind starring B.J. was not a movie where the star of the show lost a job. He became so confused by his experience that he went to see a psychologist who helped him retrain his brain to write a new mental script. The new movie said the corporate bosses made the decision to lay off their workers. It was not B.J.'s fault. It was not because of his performance (or lack thereof). Learning his new script gave him a new confidence, a new energy, and eventually, a new job.

Sometimes you become depressed and discouraged because circumstances occur that go against your mental playbook. You need to make sure your mind script allows for those things. When something bad happens in your life, do a quick rewrite. In the movie industry, script doctors are often hired to rewrite a script that is not working. Well, if your script is not working, be your own script doctor. Rewrite your story to use your challenges in a beneficial way. Create a positive reason for your failure—and then move on so your brain circuitry does not become your enemy. Because if you allow the old scenario to become a failure scenario, the movie in your mind will keep playing; and every time you try to break out, that movie will call you back. You need a new script when negative things happen; you need a new movie.

Whenever I encounter an unexpected situation, I use a Bible verse to rewrite my script: "And we know that in all things God works for the good of those who love Him, who have been called according to His purpose" (Romans 8:28 NIV). This promise from God always adjusts my mental script with a reassurance that God loves me and will always fulfill His plan for my life. That is a script I can happily live with.

8. The Remodeled Brain

Through your input (whether positive or negative), you are remodeling the circuitry of your mind; therefore, you need to recycle everything that happens to you into a positive situation. You need to reconstruct and reprocess, no matter what happens. Take every experience and mentally convert those into something helpful. If you learn to do this every time, you will train your brain to do it automatically for you. You can become the most positive thinker in the world with this technique. You will see possibilities where other people see obstacles. You will see potential where others see the unachievable. Training your brain to look for the good in every circumstance will improve your chances for success.

Some of you may be asking, "What do these negative and positive brain tracks have to do with training my brain?" I am so glad you asked. Your brain has had plenty of time to develop its negative circuitry. And now you need to lay some new tracks, which you do by incorporating into your life the ideas I presented in the positive brain tracks. You need to retrain your brain by thinking happy positive thoughts, by analyzing yourself (if you are an underperformer, find out why you are underperforming), by attaching yourself to a worthy role model, and by remodeling and recycling your experiences.

However, you must be patient. Your brain chemistry, working with your deep limbic system, may have been negatively trained for years. So it may produce emotions that will make you feel as if you do not want to change, even though you are not living the life you want. Your brain is creating emotions to reinforce where you are and who you think you are. If you do not want that, you have to take command; you have to declare war on whatever is holding you back. The good news is, it works! You can retrain your brain.

The Bible says, "Finally ... whatever is true, whatever is noble, whatever is right, whatever is pure, whatever is lovely, whatever is admirable—if anything is excellent or praiseworthy—think about such things" (Philippians 4:8 NIV). The apostle Paul, inspired by God, wrote this before anybody knew about the brain's circuits and chemical reactions. He wrote this before scientists and researchers knew how the brain operated and before they knew how to reroute neural pathways. You might be held back by thinking patterns you do not even know you have developed. Note the same Bible verse in The Living Bible: "As I close this letter let me say one more thing: Fix your thoughts on what is true and good and right. Think about things that are pure and lovely, and dwell on the fine, good things in others. Think about all you can praise God for and be glad about."

The Bible is telling you to do what the research has proven: Get your brain train on a right track, then stay on a right track long enough to alter your circuitry and create new pathways. Get on the right track and be patient. Take enough time to get the neurological pathways rewired so that your brain reinforces your thinking. Your success will then become easier because your brain circuitry will back up the new, positive person you now believe you are.

Chapter 4

The Performance Explosion

Your brain is the most important ingredient for your success. When you understand how it works, and when you begin to train it, you can dramatically improve your performance. You have learned many facts about your remarkable brain, but now you need to apply that knowledge to your life.

A few years ago, I experienced a slowdown. I still had a strong hunger to succeed and a deep desire to pursue God's purpose, but I had landed on a professional plateau; I was stuck. As I prayed and sought counsel, I realized that I needed something to create a performance explosion.

The turning point came while I was taking a walk with my wife, Amy. I was expressing my frustration when she stopped and told me she believed God had already given the answer in the brain research I was conducting.

It was an awakening. I saw that the brain-training information I had been researching held the key to unlocking my performance and pushing me forward.

You may be in a similar place. You may want more meaning and personal success; you may want a life that is far better than anything you have ever encountered, but you are stuck and unable to advance. I want to show you how brain training can elevate your life, and I will begin by opening your mind to the possibility of an extraordinary personal performance that I call having a performance explosion. High performance leadership, activity, and action are available to you right now. The pathway to the fulfillment of your dream is here. All you need to do is understand how to have a performance explosion.

A young man was driving across the country and brainstorming about an idea. He wanted to do something so big that it would rock his world; it would shake up everything about his life. During that long trip, he examined all his options, all the possibilities, and he thought, "How can I make this a reality? How can I create something so fantastic it will change my whole life?" He had already accumulated $300,000 of personal capital (money he borrowed from his parents), so he had something to work with. But his idea was so huge, he knew $300,000 would only be a drop in the bucket; he needed something far beyond that. He decided he would approach certain individuals, and he would ask them to invest some of their money so that his dream could come true.

He knew he would have to be convincing, so he came up with an approach that absolutely revolutionized his persuasive techniques. He decided that he would tell these investors: "Here, I have $300,000. I want you to come with me. What we will do is...," and he came up with three magical words—ones that will fire your blood when you hear them. He said, "With your money, my money, this idea, and my hard work, we will create something so wonderful, we will GET BIG FAST."

And with those three simple words, he sold several investors on his idea and raised the $1 million he needed. His concept of getting big fast fired them up. They did not want something that would drag on for years, which might or might not make a profit. The whole idea of getting big fast became the cornerstone of this young man's presentation, and it dazzled his financial backers.

He also wanted a big name for his new idea. After much thought, he decided that he would use the name of one of the great rivers of the world—a gigantic waterway that would represent the size of his idea. Today, Amazon.com (the world's largest online retailer) is worth billions of dollars; it is a tremendous success story. But it never would have happened if Jeff Bezos had not come up with the idea of being persuasive with three simple words: GET BIG FAST.

Now, what about you? Would you like to get big fast? Would you like something to speed up your success, something to punch you into orbit? I will explain how that can happen for you, and I am so excited because this really works.

The National Aeronautic and Space Administration (NASA) says when it launches a rocket into outer space, it takes 70 percent of the fuel for takeoff. Once the rocket is launched, it is on its way to a distant target; but it takes 70 percent of its fuel to get it off the ground.

You are like a rocket, though some of you are still sitting on the ground—rockets that have not yet blasted off. You may have a job, a position, or an idea. You may even dabble in certain business opportunities, but you have not taken off. You have not gotten big fast. Your performance explosion is what will thrust you into the outer reaches of your dreams and aspirations. Isn't that exciting?

Now, when you think about the 70 percent, at first it seems wasteful—the rocket uses almost three quarters of the fuel just to get off the ground. Well, that is true of you. You need a huge amount of knowledge, effort, and belief to get off the ground; but once you have launched, you can hit your target because the momentum will propel you where you want to go.

So do not feel bad about what it takes to get started. Do not worry about what it takes to get moving, because once you are hurtling through space, your rocket will reach the moon of your dreams. If it takes all that fuel, let it go. Let it launch; let it explode to get you going.

Once you have decided you want to get big fast, once you know you are willing to burn your fuel now to move to where you want to go, you will want to understand what an explosion performance will do in your life. I will get to the secret of how to create it, but for now I want you to realize that it is worth the effort.

Many people fail to launch their rockets because of the Meatball Theory, which says that most people secretly suspect they are meatballs. They want to be prime steak but fear they are just ordinary ground beef. They may say they are not. They may hope they are not, and they may occasionally believe they are not. But deep down inside, they fear they are nothing but another meatball. And for most, there is a deep and burning desire to become more. Those are the men and women who will look for something better, who will hope someone will open the door to something wonderful that can change their lives. Those are the ones who will go to a motivational seminar, buy an inspirational book, or start a business on the basis of their entrepreneurial commitment. Those are the people who suspect they might be meatballs but do not want to be meatballs any longer.

Please do not think I am insulting you. The fear of being a "meatball" is just another way of saying many people do not have the confidence to take a risk and reach for something higher in life. They lack the self-esteem to know they can be more than they are. Let me tell you right now: You are not a meatball; you can be more.

But, it means you will have to find some way to launch your rocket, some way to create thrust, some way to get off the ground. Something will need to happen to push you (create forward movement) into a better future. That is what I call your performance explosion.

An explosion is usually accompanied by a loud noise, and many times it is startling and shocking, which is what needs to happen in your life. You need something startling and shocking, something unexpected. You need something that will amaze your friends. When you have a performance explosion, you will have a K-A-B-O-O-M (an acronym I made up) that will launch your rocket and get you off the ground. You need this KABOOM, and you need it now. But what does the performance explosion do for you? That is what I want you to focus on.

Why is your KABOOM important? There are six reasons it is important:

1. It KEEPS you on the right track with clear goals.

Specific, attainable goals point you in the right direction and guide your decisions; they keep you on track. It is so easy to go through the normal challenges and responsibilities of everyday living and lose track of what you ought to be doing to get your "rocket launched and into orbit." You spend days, weeks, months, even years waiting for something to launch you, and the launch never occurs because you do not create the explosion. When you let the KABOOM happen, you eliminate detours and diversions. It will keep you on the right path.

2. It APPLIES the right positive principles to your life.

It is not enough to know positive principles; you have to believe them and use them. Application of the right principles will keep you from getting swamped by the negative so you do not get blown away by wrong thinking. Your performance explosion is vital because it applies the right positive principles to your life and keeps them in play until you get where you want to be.

3. It makes you BETTER.

Your KABOOM will make you dissatisfied remaining who you are, the way you are. You will want to mature and develop yourself. You will want to become better: a better student, salesperson, persuader, communicator, man or woman, wife or husband, mom or dad. Your KABOOM will leave you with a commitment to grow and improve, to learn something new and helpful (never think you know enough). It will get you out of your old life (your ruts) and launch your rocket. Your KABOOM makes you better, which is why it is so important.

4. It helps you OVERCOME your obstacles.

A good friend of mine (an older, wealthy businessman I have admired for years) told me that in his twenties and even going into his early thirties, there were many dumb things he did that cost him money. "I had to make deliberate decisions to overcome my weak tendencies," he said. "I believed people too quickly. I got in deals I never should have gotten into. I lost money because I thought a partner would take care of something when I was an absentee owner and investor." He continued, "I have learned so much. I am rich, but

I could have been a lot richer if I had just conquered those weaknesses earlier."

Your performance explosion will help you overcome your obstacles. There are things in your way, and you keep slamming against a wall. You get up; you get going, and you think, I will be better. I will have an explosion. I will change my business and my income. But what happens? Ten days later, you are still in your rut; nothing has changed. You bump into obstructions and fall back.

This has happened to me more than once. I had a real issue with something in my personal approach to business—I was disorganized. In fact, my biggest challenge every month was not paying my bills; it was finding them. I would lose them the day they arrived. I would take things and toss them aside. I would put notes in the bottom of tissue boxes and then forget where I had put them. (There was a passport renewal form I needed to send in before going on an important international trip. I took the forms, the photos, and the check, which I was going to send in, and thought, "Oh, I won't do it today. I'll put it here and send it later." To this day, I have not found that application. I had to get a new set of forms, photos, and check.) I had to make a decision that I needed an explosion, a KABOOM. I needed something that would alter the way I did things. My sloppy organization was a huge barrier to my success. It had to be mastered.

You may have something like that in your life. Maybe

it is your temper or the way you deal with people. Maybe you do not follow up. Maybe you are afraid to talk to people. Your list of road blocks and inadequacies could be three miles long. But the right performance explosion, the right KABOOM in your life will obliterate those hurdles and help you get beyond your failings. Are you ready for this? Can you imagine how good you could be and what you could accomplish if you did not have that stuff pulling you back and dragging you down? Well, the KABOOM can help you overcome your weaknesses and obstacles.

One of the richest, most successful men I know once told me he had risen to the top of his profession because he was willing to fight for his success. He trusted God to give him the strength to overcome obstacles.

5. It OPENS your mind to your real possibilities.

Some of you do not know what you can do because you do not see a vision of what you can become. You do not know how big you can get because you have a limited view of yourself. You need something (an explosion maybe?) to shock you, to shake up your world so you can understand the real possibilities of what you can do and who you can become. You have the potential to go far beyond those little changes you expect right now. Your KABOOM opens your mind to what you can become—but you must be receptive and willing to work. To improve your life, you must be teachable; you must be open to others who can instruct and guide you. (This is especially true of men, who often refuse counsel and direction and so miss their greatest opportunities.) Your KABOOM will open up opportunities, and it will open your mind to the possibilities of what you can do.

6. It launches you into a realm of life where you MATTER.

Your KABOOM can give meaning to your life. It can give you a worthy purpose. I have a good friend in California, a billionaire and wonderful Christian, who owns a high-end real estate investment management and development company. He is a remarkable individual, but what impresses me when I am with him is how much he wants to matter for God. He lives in Beverly Hills and has a desire to influence his Hollywood neighbors. People come to his home for Bible studies and support. What amazes me is not his wealth, his houses, or his private jet. What impresses me is what this man does (with his money and influence) for God. He gives to godly causes, and he makes a difference all over the world. He lives a life that has meaning and that fuels his performance explosion.

Now, I am not saying you need three billion dollars to matter. I am saying you can matter more than you matter now. You can make more of a difference than you do now. If you get your rocket launched, you can make a difference in your community, church, school system, and local politics. You can become an influential person—if you get your rocket off the pad and headed to where you are supposed to be in your life. You need a worthy purpose, and your performance explosion can give you one.

You need a KABOOM (a performance explosion) in your life, which will do what Jeff Bezos talked about in his promotion of Amazon. A performance explosion has the power to get you there and to get big quick, but you need something that will ignite it.

Chapter 5

The Amygdala Secret

All explosions need an ignition. And the greatest ignition secret I have discovered in all of my research is something so simple, it is embedded in your biology. (It is also the greatest motivational, communication, and performance secret.)

Earlier, I talked about how the brain can be programmed to be positive, how it can create its own positive neurological circuits to support you in your success.

Well, if you want this explosion to occur—and I know you want it—the mystery of motivating and exploding your life with a performance explosion is what I call The Amygdala Secret.

The Bible says we are "fearfully and wonderfully made [by God]" (Psalm 139:14 NIV), and what He has done in your brain is phenomenal.

Now, let's look at the amygdala for a moment. It is not exactly a specific organ, but rather a collection—and I am oversimplifying this dramatically—a series of neural pathways at the lower back base of the brain. It is a key component of the deep limbic system of the human brain and the trigger point for all emotional response. It is one of the few areas of the brain that functions from birth.

Why does that matter to you now? Because the amygdala is the source of your emotion, and what you are emotional about, you will do. The amygdala can be the source of depression and mood swings, but it also can be the source of great positive emotion.

Liz Phelps, director of the Phelps Laboratory of New York University, says "[the amygdala] has been called the seat of emotion." It is the part of your brain that not only creates an emotional response but also is affected by the emotions you allow it to develop.

The amygdala is the secret to your rocket launch, your performance explosion. So how does it work? It is not some mysterious, mystical thing. It is not something that controls you; you can control it. But the amygdala is so powerful and so quick in its ability to create emotion that you need to understand how it operates so you can learn to manage it. The amygdala is so fast that it enables you to size up an object or situation and have an emotional response toward it in one and a half seconds.

For example, you are watching television and a

commercial comes on. In one and a half seconds, you can form an impression of someone or something in that ad. You form an emotional response just like that.

In fact, the amygdala is so fast that when you listen to a speaker, you will know if you like that speaker in a second and a half. A jury will often decide what they think about a particular case during the opening remarks by the lawyer, based on their emotional response to that lawyer. That is before they have heard the evidence or examined the case.

Why is this important? Your rocket launch is related to your amygdala because what ignites your emotions ignites you. I know you think of yourself as a logical person, but you are much more emotional than you realize. Your amygdala is so fast in evaluating something emotionally that its influence is already pushing you before your logical mind even gets going. I am not discounting the importance of logic, and I am not discounting the importance of facts. You need both. In fact, I believe most of us do not think enough. But, if you are going to get yourself moving, you have to start with the amygdala because whatever ignites your emotions ignites you.

A medical doctor told me that when it comes to your brain's decision-making, you are like a charioteer riding in an old-world chariot pulled by two animals. These animals represent parts of your brain: Your careful, logical reasoning power and your amygdala (the emotional source).

He said it would be like running your chariot with a pony and an elephant: The pony representing your reasoning and the elephant representing your emotion. An elephant is much bigger than a pony, which means your emotions are much more prominent in your decision-making than your logic.

Now again, do not misunderstand. I am not telling you that logic is unimportant, nor am I telling you to forego research. But human beings are emotional; emotions are at the root of their decisions. So if you want to launch your rocket, you have to get excited. You must engage your emotions; you must stimulate your amygdala.

I know an engineer who is very methodical, rational, and factual. He is difficult to talk to because he is so uninterested in anything emotional. I needed his help on a project I was working on (I could not move forward without his input), but nothing I said connected with him.

I had almost given up; until one day, something finally clicked. We were talking about the project; there was some technical detail related to his field of interest, which I stumbled into by accident. It was something he was passionate about, and he instantly changed. I could see it; I could sense it. This indifferent, technology-driven engineer had an emotional response toward that one small segment of his research. His amygdala was engaged, and he began talking in a more animated way. This man's rational side was strong; but I found that to get him interested enough to talk, I had to focus on that detail that created an amygdala response.

After this small connection, I was able to guide his emotions so that he became much more open to the idea I was presenting. I had been trying to communicate with him for years through the use of heavy logic and facts. But once I connected to his amygdala, I was able to give him information that supported his passion; and he responded warmly and excitedly. Within fifteen minutes, he agreed to join the project. It was an "amygdala moment."

Thinking is not easy. Research has discovered that most people dislike thinking because it is painful. I do not mean physically painful, but the mental strain is difficult. Deep thought burns about 300 calories per hour, so it is an effort, which is why most people rely on their amygdala (their emotional response, their gut instinct) to make decisions. Because of the effort involved, most do not take the time to consider the logic of what is presented. So if you can connect emotionally with them, you have opened the door to reason (intellect). The logic does not come first; the emotion does.

For many years, you may have wondered why your rocket has not launched. You may have come up with a long list of why you need to change your life, why you need to do better, why you need to make more money, or why your job is not working; but nothing gets your rocket off the ground. And do you know why? You have not stimulated your amygdala. You have tried the intellectual route (which has value), but it is your emotions that open your mind to facts and reason.

Adolf Hitler was a brilliant communicator who manipulated people's emotions. He knew how to rouse their amygdala responses, bringing them into evil. Rationality was thrown out the window—which is not what I am telling you to do. Do you want your rocket to launch? Do you want to get big fast? Then you need to have your emotions aroused. You need to feel passion pouring through your life. You need to excite your amygdala.

There is another thing you need to know about the amygdala. It evaluates two things in making a decision: credibility and likeability.

A man came to see me. After we sat down, he said, "I am a committed Christian who goes to church. I love my wife. I have never been unfaithful or unkind to her, and yet she says she doesn't trust me." I immediately wanted to speak to his wife, so I arranged an interview. The wife turned out to be a down-to-earth, likeable individual who was committed to God, her husband, and children. She told me she loved her husband but agreed that she did not trust him. I asked her, "Does your husband lie to you?"

"Well, that depends on what you mean by lying," she answered.

"Has he ever been unfaithful? Does he trick you?"

"He's not unfaithful; but again, it depends on what you mean by tricking."

I was intrigued. "Explain what you're saying."

"My husband isn't credible. When he says something, he embellishes it; he exaggerates. My husband has an excitable personality. He's outgoing, artistic, and entertaining. He's very sanguine, very inspiring, but he overstates things. He adds to the mix. He doesn't quite give an accurate view of something. Over the years, I've learned not to trust what he says. He'll tell me some big story, and I have learned to shake my head and say, 'That's just my husband.'"

I brought the husband in to listen to this evaluation. He was distressed, "I try to tell the truth. I don't mean anything bad." It is true; he did not mean anything bad. But she had observed him, and now, her amygdala responded instantly to anything he brought up. His credibility was questioned because he exaggerated and because he was evasive; he could not be pinned down on things. It took a surprisingly long time, more counseling and prayer together than I had expected, before he finally stopped what he was doing so his wife could trust him again. If you want to receive a positive amygdala response, you must not do anything that creates a lack of credibility or trust. Jesus said it this way, "But let your 'Yes' be 'Yes,' and your 'No,' 'No'." (Matthew 5:37 NKJV) In other words, do not play games with words. The amygdala immediately assesses credibility and likeability; so you do not want to do anything that undermines your credibility, even in the smallest way.

The same is true of likeability. I have a friend who is a health-care professional. He is a committed Christian who genuinely cares about others. The problem is he has a gruff way that is intimidating. He is difficult to work with; he does not suffer fools gladly, and he shows it. Even though he is a caring person, he turns people off because of the negative amygdala response he creates. He has had to soften his approach so his patients will respond well to him.

So, I encourage you to use the knowledge of the amygdala to launch your own rocket. But I also encourage you to use it as a way to help other people get their rockets launched. You need to be an amygdala communicator and persuader. If you want to motivate other people to follow you, you must reach them on their amygdalae level because it opens their mind and yours. Use the amygdala as a way to connect with others so they will listen to your intellectual thoughts with a responsive mind. (Remember, people are functioning with a pony and an elephant—and the emotional elephant usually wins.) Whatever ignites other people's emotions ignites them. So, if you are going to influence people, you need to reach them through their amygdalae. And you cannot do that if your credibility and likeability are tarnished.

Do you ever feel as if you are partially paralyzed in your efforts to succeed? Do you feel as if sometimes you are swimming in a sea of molasses? Do you find it hard to move through the syrupy mess that is your life? The reason you feel this way could be because of your amygdala. Let me explain.

Your amygdala is vital to your launch. You already know that your emotions trigger your performance explosion because what ignites your emotions ignites you. Your emotions provide the energy (fuel) that creates the rocket blast-off. So, let's say you get to where you know your launch needs to happen: You know you need to improve your bank account; you know you need to make changes to get different results in your life. You are now ready to launch your rocket. Your amygdala is fired up, and your emotions are pouring in. You are ready to go, go, go.

When you decide to do something, your amygdala responds with immediate emotional support. (Think about how you feel when you first become excited about doing something. You are flooded with feelings of enthusiasm.)

But what happens if you fail to follow through? What happens if you say, "Hey, I'll wait on changing this habit"? What happens when you admit, "Yes, I need to take care of that financial problem, but I'll wait and deal with it later"? Your amygdala is a delicate mechanism in your brain process, and it is sensitive to delay. The word WAIT is deadly to its operation. The moment you wait, all momentum goes away. The moment you say wait, your emotions die, your motivation fades, and your launch is aborted.

In a similar way that brain fog creates confusion, your amygdala can become confused by the mixed signals you are sending by your indecision. Why does this happen? Your amygdala has been stimulated and engaged. Your emotions are pouring through your brain circuits giving you the push (thrust) to launch, but when you say wait, your amygdala backs off. The emotions drop and the logical brain takes over: You begin to examine your decision. (Yes, there are decisions that need examining to keep you from doing something stupid. I am not talking about those.) Your amygdala has gotten involved, and your emotions are pouring.

If you say wait, you become a chronic re-analyzer, a chronic re-appraiser. Waiting will paralyze you. Your momentum will shift from the emotional part of your brain to the logical part, which will then provide reasons not to launch your rocket. Your emotions, which were so aroused at first, are now gone, and your logical mind has to come up with why they are gone.

Since your amygdala has become emotionally confused by your hesitation, your cerebral cortex takes over; it is doing what it thinks it should. It says you should not go for it; you should not launch your rocket.

If you suddenly stop your launch, your cerebral cortex will offer the rationale why waiting is the right thing to do; and it will be much harder to re-launch—which is why WAIT is such a deadly word to your amygdala.

So the reason you feel like you are swimming in

molasses could be because of that word WAIT. The moment you think it, the moment you say it, you pull the plug on your launch; you keep your rocket rusting on the pad. When you allow this word to win, your amygdala is bypassed and something happens that aborts your performance explosion. That is the way the amygdala and the logical mind play off one another.

Your amygdala can pour out massive positive and negative emotions. It is the seat of moods and depression, so it can create floods of detrimental emotion that will overwhelm you and keep you from accomplishing anything—which is why it is vital you feed it positive stimulants. To launch your rocket (life), you will need your amygdala on your side.

So as part of your brain training, you must develop this small section of your brain. You must nourish it with the right stimulators, the right igniters. How you think and what you do will feed your amygdala and create the response you need to get launched. Here is a list of amygdala stimulators, which, incidentally, also positively train your brain:

1. Inspirational Movies
These are films that arouse you on an amygdala level and motivate you to change your life. I have always been inspired by the Rocky movies. These films bypass my reason and go right to my emotions; they create an immediate response. When I watch Rocky Balboa running in the predawn hours in Philadelphia, with the Rocky theme surging in the background, I am moved.

When he tells his manager to, "Cut me, Mick" (because his eye is swollen and he wants to continue the fight), I feel his passion.

There are many films today that are cynical; they mock success and inspiration. You need to avoid those because they will negatively affect your amygdala. You are constantly programming your amygdala to respond, so make sure you watch things that inspire and motivate you.

I still remember the movie, *Chariots of Fire*, about the 1924 Olympics in Paris. I watch it and still get a lump in my throat. This film is based on Eric Liddell, a Scottish runner, who surprised the world with his grace and courage as he won a gold medal in track and field. It is the story of a man who placed his Christian convictions (about not running on a Sabbath day) ahead of competition. His example continues to inspire people today. Inspirational films activate an amygdala response. These movies encourage you to be a better person; they inspire you to do great things and overcome difficult odds.

2. Motivational Books

I read a fascinating book by Larry McMurtry, *Books: A Memoir*, on book-collecting that was well-written, intriguing, and informative. Toward the end, he writes of his concern we may be producing a non-reading generation (I worry about that too).

Reading stimulates certain neural pathways in the

brain like nothing else does. We dare not lose our capacity to think. I know I do not want to lose my capacity to think, especially as it concerns my faith, which is important to me. (I want to be an intellectually sound Christian, a thinker.) You need motivational books—ones that lift your spirit and encourage your heart. This is vital for you, your children, and grandchildren. You need books that feed your amygdala, books that fire you up and improve your life. Read biographies of men and women who accomplished great deeds and blessed the lives of others. My life has grown because of reading about Theodore Roosevelt, Abraham Lincoln, Ronald Reagan, Billy Graham, and John Wesley. These wise individuals have taught me lessons in humility and service.

3. Uplifting Music

There are many kinds of musical forms available: country, rock, contemporary Christian, classical, jazz, rhythm and blues. Some elevate and some depress.

I encountered a man who told me that when he visited a dance club in New York City, he listened to music so depressing he had thoughts of desperation. In her book *Hole In Our Soul: The Loss of Beauty and Meaning in American Popular Music*, Martha Bayles warns about the negative emotional effects of jarring, heavy music filled with harsh, ugly lyrics. She writes that some music can put a "hole in your soul."

In contrast, music that makes you happy and lyrics that inspire your heart connect to your amygdala and create a positive response. If you want to launch your rocket, you need your amygdala 100 percent on your side; thus, you need to feed it the right food (the right stimulation), which includes uplifting music.

4. Supportive Friends

You need friends who support your dreams. If they do not support your desire to be bigger and better than you have ever been, then they are not true friends. Do not allow the wrong people to influence your life. Your peer group is enormously influential on your amygdala. If your conscious mind hears negative, unsupportive comments from your so-called friends, your amygdala immediately responds and creates an emotional reaction, which then feeds your logical mind and makes you doubt who you are. Positive companions create a positive response from your amygdala; negative companions create a negative response.

I had a friend in college who constantly told me I was wrong to expect big things in life. One day, I returned from speaking at an off-campus event and saw this friend. I was excited about the excellent time I had enjoyed and was eager to share my blessing. When I told her about my experience, she frowned and said I was wrong to focus on success. She said it was a sign of overconfidence; I would soon learn that life was not as happy as I thought. The conversation had an immediate, depressing effect on my amygdala. I was down for days. All my pleasure at how God had blessed me evaporated.

Some time later, I realized my depression was only

the result of my friend's negative spirit. It had nothing to do with God or His will for my life. I decided I needed a different friend who would support and encourage my dreams. Do you want your amygdala to be properly programmed to help you launch? Then hang out with friends who will support you.

5. Measurable Results

Your amygdala is affected by measurable results, so you need a Daily Measurable Task (DMT) constantly programming it. A DMT makes you feel good about where you are going because it creates a response that will encourage you to persevere. Every day you need to stimulate your amygdala into releasing positive emotion that says you can be better and you can do more. Supportive emotions result from regular accomplishments, and those supportive emotions keep you going; they fuel your rocket. I do not care how rational you are; I do not care how strong your willpower is. You, a human being made by God Almighty, are fueled by emotion. And because you are fueled by emotion, you need to experience daily measurable results that will further the positive direction you want to go. A DMT will feed your amygdala and support your performance explosion.

6. Avoiding Pain

I know this seems like an odd way to stimulate your amygdala, but there is great emotional benefit in avoiding pain. Emotions are connected to pain—and I do not mean just physical suffering. There is also the embarrassment that occurs when a bill collector calls and you do not have the money. Embarrassment is painful. Not being able to pay your mortgage is painful, as is not having enough money to enroll your children in a program they dream of doing.

So, how does avoiding pain train your amygdala? You need to understand what I call the Law of Consequences —everything you do creates a consequence. There are no exceptions to this law. If you make foolish financial decisions, you suffer financial repercussions; and your amygdala reacts with the emotion of pain, which discourages and depresses you.

But, if you make good decisions (whether financially, relationally, or spiritually), the Law of Consequences works in your favor because good decisions create good outcomes. And when you have a positive outcome, you avoid pain, and your amygdala responds with supportive emotion: "I like this. I like not being in pain." So you work harder to avoid future pain. Thus, you build your business, make your phone calls, and contact your people. Your amygdala approves when you do things that avoid pain; it creates emotion that will facilitate the avoidance of more pain, making it easier to launch your rocket.

7. Fantastic Fantasies
This is just another way of saying you need big, dynamic, wonderful dreams. When you pursue fantastic fantasies, your amygdala gets excited and gives you emotional support, making it easier to reach your aspirations.

Steve Jobs (Apple, Inc. co-founder and CEO who passed away in 2011) would often refer to what he called reality distortion fields. The term was invented by an Apple employee, but Mr. Jobs used it to describe his approach to innovation. When Steve Jobs gave speeches about a reality distortion field, he wanted his listeners to think of some possibility in their future that could distort their current reality, something that would shake them up, shock them. He said he wanted them to have dreams so big, so great, they would be jarred to the bone. They would think, "Wow, how amazing that would be. What a fantastic fantasy if that were to come true." So pursue big dreams, not little ones. Your amygdala loves to pour emotion into something exciting, and you need emotion to do the job.

Once you have dreamed your big dreams, write a detailed diary (for a week) of what your life will be like when they come true. Create your own reality distortion field by writing a journal based on what you believe can happen. This will distort your current reality because you will be focusing on your possibilities. The future shakes up the now and stirs the amygdala, which then creates the emotion that helps you succeed. That is why I call this an amygdala igniter. Future fantasies create hope, and the amygdala feeds on hope. It pumps positive emotion because of the hope you focus on in your possible future.

8. Understanding Family

I know many of you have been disappointed, frustrated, and angered by the failure of your spouses to come through when they promised to improve the life of the family. But when you dump your criticism and belittlement on them, their amygdalae get programmed to produce emotions that support the negative you are punching into them. Your verbal assault creates an amygdala drop that makes it much more difficult for them to succeed.

Wives, you need to believe in your husbands. Even if they have not proven themselves, support them. You will only make matters worse by convincing them they are losers. Your encouragement can improve their opinion of themselves, which will stimulate their amygdalae to create the emotions that will boost them up.

This also applies to husbands and parents. Husbands, you need to love and encourage your wives. Parents, you need to support and cherish your children.

9. Good Time Management

You need to live on the principle of sooner rather than later. When I was younger, I had a problem with procrastination. I graduated high school with a C average because I always put off writing my papers until the week they were due. My grades the first term in college were two Ds, a C, and an F. I was put on academic probation and sent to a remedial reading class at a local elementary school. I was eighteen years old—and I had to attend a class with nine- and ten-year-olds to learn how to read. Reading was not my problem (I had been reading since I was four years old; and by the time I was eleven, I was reading 300 books a year), but I still had to go through the embarrassment of attending class with those elementary kids. The experience so shook me, I became more serious about college; I stopped procrastinating. After I graduated, I was accepted into graduate school, where I made almost all As.

Use time to your advantage. Your amygdala responds to now, which is why I said earlier that wait is such a deadly word. When you procrastinate, your amygdala shuts down and your cerebral cortex takes over by coming up with reasons you should procrastinate; your amygdala then reengages to supply the emotions that reinforce your procrastination. It is a self-defeating cycle.

Create urgency and deadlines. And when you create a deadline, back it up. Do what you are supposed to do; follow through. Make use of good time management to convince your amygdala you are serious about your goals.

10. Dynamic Duo: DUTY and DIGNITY

A married couple came for counseling. The husband, a serial procrastinator, had created problems because he did not take time to manage their finances. He did not like balancing their checkbook or monitoring their bills. He did not like working hard to make more money—so he did none of it. His loyal, sweet wife was hurt and resentful because of their financial difficulties.

I remember one counseling session when he turned to his wife and asked, "Well, sweetheart, what can I do to change?" She looked at him and said, "You know, you've promised to change so many times. You've promised you'll be better; you'll be different. I don't believe it anymore." She paused, "Grow up; be a real man for once. If you did that, maybe things would change." The blood drained from his face; he was stricken because she had nailed his real problem: He was a spoiled kid who had not grown up. When he didn't want to do something, he didn't do it. As a result, their marriage was suffering, and their finances were in trouble.

The couple came back about eight months later, and the husband was a different person. This whole idea of doing his duty (I'm the leader of this family; they depend on me to provide for them) had reached his soul and transformed him. He loved fulfilling his responsibilities; and he loved the dignity, the self-respect, he gained.

The dynamic duo of Duty and Dignity made him into a real man, and his amygdala poured out positive, supportive emotions. He loved who he had become, and he never looked back—and his wife was more in love with him than ever. It saved their marriage.

Do the right thing and do it now. Your self-esteem will soar, and your amygdala will create emotions that will make you feel so good about yourself your rocket will launch.

Chapter 6

The Effective Communicator
(Part 1)

All right, your rocket is launched. It is off the pad, hurtling towards your goal. You have blasted off on the way to your new future. Now that you are in flight, there are certain things that will help you get to your ultimate destination, and one of those is what I call being an amygdala communicator.

So much of life depends upon your ability to persuade other people of your viewpoint, your idea, your dream, your business model, or whatever. Your ability to be a persuader is critical to your success.

You have already learned that the amygdala is the seat of emotions. Understanding how this emotion-based component of your brain works can help you communicate more effectively with others—which is why we have spent time studying it. By connecting to the amygdalae (the emotional core, the heart and soul) of other people, you are on your way to being a better communicator and persuader.

There are three elements to effective communication: preparation, connection, and conclusion. In this chapter, I will deal with the first two: I will teach you how to prepare to win, and then I will examine how to connect with others so they will like you and want to work with you.

The third element—how to bring it to a conclusion that will create a response (an action) and a commitment to pursue what you have persuaded them to do—will be covered in the next chapter.

The first element of good amygdala communication is PREPARATION, which begins before you ever meet another person. And the main purpose of preparation is to lower your tension. You need to lower your tension as much as possible so your amygdala does not react to the stress and produce negative emotions. If you want the emotional support of your amygdala, you need to eliminate as many unknowns as possible. You do this in several ways:

1. Scope out the logistics ahead of time
If you are unorganized and unsure, your amygdala will respond to your stressed mindset and send negative emotions that match your mental state. The best way to manage this is to organize your approach and plan what you want to say and do.

Imagine that you have arranged a business appointment with someone. If you want the positive emotional support of your amygdala, then you should eliminate tension by confirming the address, checking the route, and leaving early so you will not be pressured by time. If you do not prepare (you do not know where the person lives; you do not check your route in advance, or you run behind schedule), you will arrive at your appointment late and flustered—not a great start to your business meeting. And because you are flustered, your amygdala will be pumping negative emotions, which will make it harder to perform. Your anxiety will create an immediate response. Before your knuckles ever knock on the door, your amygdala will produce condemning emotions that will make it more difficult for you to communicate.

So eliminate tension by scoping out the logistics ahead of time. Circle the block; get an idea of your contact's neighborhood, house, yard, and car. This will relax you because it will give you an opportunity to evaluate the person before your scheduled meeting.

If the appointment is at a restaurant, get there early; look for a table away from any competing noise. Find a location where you will not be distracted.

I spoke with a man who said the single biggest mistake he made in going to a business appointment was not arriving early enough to check out the restaurant. He had scheduled to meet a client (one with a great deal of potential) at a restaurant to present a business plan. And because he could not scope out the restaurant ahead of time, the hostess put them by the doorway to the kitchen. He said during the entire meeting, as he tried to discuss business, the kitchen door would open and close; servers would walk in and out, clinking and rattling their dishes. Whenever the door opened, he heard the noise of the kitchen. He and the potential client had the worst table in the house. He said his whole appointment was so disrupted that he never got on track. Although they left in a friendly manner, he never closed the deal. So if you want to eliminate sources of tension, arrive early— whether it is at a restaurant, home, or neutral location.

You never know what you might encounter. I once heard a quote from a person who grew up in a Marine Corps family. She said her parents taught her the saying, "Two is one and one is none". Always have a backup in case the first item does not work. Whenever she had an exam, she would repeat this as a reminder to take two pencils to the test site in case one broke. If you want to give a brochure or catalog to the prospective client, take two brochures, two catalogs. If you plan to leave a CD with him, take two. You may misplace one, or you may accidentally sit on one in the car. If you are going to take notes, have two notebooks and two pens. One may run out of ink or stop working. Two is one, and one is none.

You want to increase your odds of not having little things be a source of tension. And it is amazing how little things can create stress: a pen that does not work, a pencil that breaks, or a CD that is not in the folder. So make sure you are prepared. Do whatever you can to eliminate specific sources of tension, which will help your amygdala respond in a positive manner.

2. Dress appropriately

It is always a good idea to be a little better dressed than the person you are meeting. I did not say be much better dressed. I did not say be better dressed to the point you are blowing him out of the water with how great you look. Just be a little better dressed. If you are going to meet in casual clothes, then wear a nice shirt. Do not wear anything wrinkled or shabby. (You may be younger and more used to people who are informally dressed with baggy pants and untucked shirttails, which are fine for going to a ball game or out with friends for buffalo wings; but they will not make a positive business impression.)

You do not have to overdo it; you do not have to be overly formal. But make sure you are dressed appropriately and just a step ahead of where you think the other person is. You are always in a leadership position; so if you are only slightly ahead, then you are not embarrassing him on any level. Tension is not the ally of your amygdala, which works best under stress-free conditions when your emotions can flow in a positive way. Good preparation involves being appropriately dressed.

3. Plan your conversation

Many people worry about what they will say to another person and how well they will say it. If you are speaking with someone you do not know and want to make a good impression, focus on why you want to speak to the person. Find a specific reason you want to talk to him before you ever arrive at the meeting. It needs to be a reason that will create a positive emotional response in the individual: "I know you want to make more money"; or "I've been playing golf with you, so I know you love to play. I bet you would like more time on the course." When planning your conversation, focus on a good reason you think he would respond to you. Tailor your remarks, your plan, or your business approach to what you think he would find appealing. Oh ... and do not forget to practice. Rehearsing what you will say will eliminate tension.

4. Put yourself in his place

Good preparation will allow you to see the situation from his perspective, which will calm you and better engage your amygdala. Try to imagine how he might respond to you. What do you think you look like to him? If you were he, what would interest you? The more you understand the other individual, the more relaxed you will be. And the more relaxed you are, the better your amygdala response. Put yourself in his position and imagine, "If I were he, with what little I know about him, what would I want out of a meeting like this?" The person is probably nervous, maybe even a little defensive. Maybe he is thinking you will try to talk him into something. So put yourself in his position. How would you feel if you were the invitee? What would be a good reason for you to respond to someone like you?

5. Ask the "what-if" questions

Something I do to lower my tension and prepare to speak with someone is use the "what-if" technique. I study the situation in advance and ask myself a series of what-if questions: What if the person is negative or hostile? (What will I do?) What if the person is late? (Do I have other work I can do?) What if the person brings someone else I do not know? (How will I interact with two people instead of the one for whom I prepared?) What if somebody interrupts us? (How will I get back on track?) What if the wife comes in and does not like what I am saying? (What will I say?) What if the individual wants to watch television the whole time I am talking? (How will I handle that?) (Most of the time, it is OK to say, "Hey, John, do you mind if we turn this off for a few minutes? I want to keep my thoughts clear." Most people will be mannerly and agree to turn it off; but you need to be prepared.) What if the person is bored with what I say? (Do I have some snappy story or interesting detail to reconnect to the client's emotions?) Do a quick examination of the possibilities of your encounter. Do not overdo it, though; do not think of every contingency. Just come up with a few main ones so you will be mentally prepared.

The "what-if" technique is endlessly adaptable. You can use it to prepare for almost any difficult possibility. When you get ready for an interview or a presentation, imagine the three worst (hostile, defensive, or mean) questions someone could ask you, then come up with answers to all three. Doing this will lower your tension level; it will relax you and enable your amygdala to produce positive emotions, which will make it easier for you to do a good job. It will also eliminate one of the most significant sources of stress: fear of the unknown.

6. Decide in advance what results you want

What do you want your client to say about you after the appointment is over? What do you want your contact to say about the presentation of your idea, dream, or business model? You may want to write down the reactions you are hoping to induce, along with the different points you can make to produce those reactions. When you finish writing, use what you have written to make a conversational plan.

This level of preparation will cause you to relax and engage your amygdala in the most positive way. And when you are well-prepared and confident, you convey that to your audience, whether it is a one-on-one meeting or a group situation. The amygdala of each person is evaluating you. It is pumping emotion into him while you are speaking. Everything you do is creating an instantaneous amygdala response in him. Thus, you want to lower stress so his amygdala causes him to like and be comfortable with you.

Everything depends on how your listener feels when he is with you. (This is true whether you have one listener or multiple listeners: Everything depends on how they feel when they are with you.)

I was in California a few years ago recording a television show on relationships. The producer of the show said,

"I want to tell you a story. I did a similar program on marriage and relationships, and I interviewed Ellen Kreidman who had written a book called, *Light His Fire: How to Keep Your Man Passionately and Hopelessly in Love With You*. We were in the middle of the broadcast when I asked her, 'What do you think is the single most important thing you can say to the women listening to you right now? All over America, women are watching this program. What is the most important advice you can give them?' She thought for a moment, then said, 'A husband is affected primarily by one thing: How he feels when he is with you. If he feels like a winner, if he feels like a giant, if he feels like a man, if he feels great about himself, he will want to be with you because you make him feel that way. If you don't make him feel that way, you have opened the door to the possibility of his finding that feeling with somebody else.'"

Then he said, "Ron, that same thing is true for you tomorrow. Everything depends, not on how the viewers feel about you, but on how they feel about themselves as they watch you. Everything depends on how your presentation makes them feel about themselves."

Reader, I want you to learn that lesson too. Remember: you want a positive amygdala response. Everything depends on how people feel when they are with you. So in your one-on-one appointment, you want to encourage and compliment your listener (for example, say good things about his family). If his amygdala pumps out emotions that make him feel good about himself, he will associate those positive emotions with you because they are occurring in the context of his conversation with you. And being well-prepared improves your chances of creating a positive amygdala response, both in you and in your listener.

The second element of good amygdala communication is CONNECTION. I want to give you eleven helpful ways to connect with another person. All decrease tension and create a positive amygdala connection.

1. Lower the sense of risk

Your invitee is already anxious: He is wondering what you want. He is wondering if your idea will cost him money. He is nervous about what his wife or friends might think if he agrees to your plan. He might have a whole collection of things that are already depressing his amygdala and bringing negative emotions. And if his amygdala is creating negative emotions, his logical mind will come up with good reasons not to work with you. But if you reassure him, if you let him know up front that there is no pressure, then you have a much better chance of connecting with him. Tell him you are just talking; you are just giving him information. It is vital you lower his sense of risk.

2. Search for similarities

To connect to the person you are meeting, search for similarities in your lives. Be like him as much as possible. Listen for things you have in common. If he likes baseball, have him predict who will win the World Series. If he likes tennis, talk about tennis. If he likes football, discuss the latest game or quarterback controversy. If he likes eating out, ask him about his favorite restaurants. If he likes fishing, get him to tell you some stories. Look for a topic that can create a rapport with him.

In psychology, there is a method of connection called physical mirroring (where you physically copy the other person), which is used to put somebody at ease. You create comfort by casually doing what he does—without being intrusive. If he crosses his legs, wait a moment before also crossing your legs. If he puts one elbow up on the table, after a moment, put your elbow on the table too. If your client is ill at ease, finding out that you have many things in common will relax him and help you make the connection you need.

3. Create a value profile

The purpose is to discover what the other person values so you can add that to your conversation. To do this, you ask, "What do you think are the three most important things in life?" He will probably answer with words like family and happiness. Most are very general when they answer this question. That is OK because the next part of the value profile makes this work.

After your person has described two or three things, ask him the next question: "How would you rate those three things by value? Which of those is number one (most important)? number two? number three?" (Always respect what the other person values, but definitely use that knowledge to form a deeper connection.) What a person values reveals what matters most to him.

I once had a conversation with someone I had never met. We were sitting in a café in Germany, and we began to talk because he spoke excellent English. I asked several questions about his country to discover any points of similarity. I even "mirrored" to make him feel more comfortable.

But when I asked him what he considered most important in his life, I received a strong emotional response. He pulled his wallet from his pocket and showed me pictures of his wife and daughters. He glowed with pride. Because I also value family, we moved into a warm and friendly discussion. Our amygdalae caused an emotional connection based on our shared values: our families. Create a value profile, which will give you a peek into the person you are meeting, so you can tailor your presentation accordingly.

4. Act as if things are easy

Numerous studies have shown that stressed behavior transfers tension to others. Nobody wants to work with someone who is agitated or distracted. You should always act calm, competent, and in control, even (especially) if you do not feel you are.

People follow leaders who are composed, capable, and commanding, or at least those who seem to be. I spoke to a woman who was in a multitasking frenzy. She was doing so many things her stress level had increased. When I asked her why she did not slow down and do fewer things, she said, "Well, I have to do everything. I have no choice." She then explained that she had twelve items on her to-do list for that morning and fifteen for the afternoon. Her busyness made her feel important, and she thought it made her seem important to other people too. But she conveyed such a sense of near panic that my amygdala immediately sent me unfavorable emotional signals about her. I am sure she did not realize she was generating such a negative response. She seemed stressed, unstable, and on edge. I was nervous to be around her.

So, if something goes wrong in your preparation (for example, you did not bring a CD you need), do not tell the other person. Make no apologies. Do not say, "I'm sorry I'm late"; or "I was going to bring a CD for you, but I forgot." It makes you look incompetent. Instead, say something like, "I know a great CD that will give you more information. I'll make sure you get it tomorrow." You see, their amygdala is constantly doing an emotional assessment of you, so appear competent, calm, and in command. Act as if things are easy.

5. Be forgiving and generous
Do not be demanding and critical. You are not there to correct his thinking or reroute his politics. We all have issues we care about. But that is not the purpose of this business lunch, professional interview, or career opportunity.

Never confuse ignorance with stupidity. Do not sit there thinking, This guy is so stupid; doesn't he understand this? She is so dumb; didn't she get it? Maybe the person does not have a background in what you are talking about. Perhaps he lacks knowledge or information or is just inexperienced. That does not make him a stupid person.

Remember: The amygdala is very intuitive and emotionally sensitive; it is possible your associate will pick up on your signals and realize you are having a negative response to him. If that is the case, his amygdala will then get into the act and create a negative emotional response toward you.

Avoid labeling someone. Do not brand the person you are meeting. Your amygdala will want to give an immediate reaction, which makes it easy to attach a label. You may think he is like this or that—and you may be right—but it will not help you connect, especially if it is something negative. So try to ignore the labeling and give the person a chance. After all, you may be wrong; your amygdala is not perfect. Train yourself to see the whole person. Jesus said, "A new command I give you: Love one another. As I have loved you, so you must love one another" (John 13:34 NIV).

I spoke in a church in Pennsylvania where the music director was bitter and angry because certain people in the congregation wanted to use a different form of worship. When I met him to plan the service, he spent the first thirty minutes warning me about those he called "the problem people."

My wife and I had dinner that evening with the leader of the "problem people." He was a kind, thoughtful individual who expressed deep love and appreciation for the music leader.

When it was time for the sermon, I spoke on love and forgiveness. God powerfully used the message, and many people responded by dedicating their lives to Christ. After praying with those who had walked to the front of the church to confirm their commitments, I began to close the service.

But before I could conclude, the music leader, who was now standing at the back, waved his hand to get my attention. Everyone stood quietly as this man labored to walk to the front, aided by a cane. He had suffered a stroke earlier in the year and struggled to move down the aisle. When he finally arrived at the front, he turned to face the audience. With tears pouring down his face, he confessed his hatred and resentment toward the people who had wanted to try a different style of worship. He then asked God's forgiveness and theirs. It was an emotional moment. Dozens of individuals, including those he had criticized, surrounded the man with hugs. It was an act of God.

Give the person you are meeting a chance. You know more than he does about your business, idea, opportunity, or concept. If he does not get it right away, go easy on him. People need love. Be forgiving and generous. Give him the same love and respect you want for yourself.

6. Understand his (or her) learning style
If your lunch companion does not comprehend your

idea, it could have more to do with how you are giving your presentation than with his lack of intelligence. You may not be giving your presentation in a learning style he uses. Not everyone has the same style of learning, because everyone learns differently. So when you explain your concept to your business contact, know which style your listener prefers. There are three styles of learning: aural (auditory), kinesthetic, and visual.

The aural learner is the one who learns by hearing words. The auditory person is so tuned into what you say and how you say it that he will focus carefully on which words you use and how you use them. If your lunch companion is an auditory learner, give a brief, clear presentation, because he will listen to every word. Do not use verbiage, because he will notice every word you say. Do not exaggerate; do not embellish.

The kinesthetic learner is more physical. He notices and learns from your body language. He is all about touch. The kinesthetic learner is someone who is hands-on, someone who learns by taking notes. The physical act of taking notes is almost as important to him as the note itself. If your business contact is a kinesthetic learner, have a notebook and pencil available for his use. Bring samples to the lunch so he has a chance to pick them up and examine them. Involve his sense of touch as much as you can.

Finally, the visual learner is the individual who responds to pictures and images. He will also watch your body language. If your meeting is with a visual learner, supply visual aids that will pique his interest. Use charts, photographs, and illustrations.

Understanding the differences between your male and female contacts will also strengthen your amygdala connections. There is a lot of information out there on men and women and their gender and temperament differences, so I will not get into detail here. But in general, when a man approaches a discussion of a business, idea, or concept, he usually approaches it in two ways: What is the point? What is the problem?

In general, a woman is aware of the atmosphere of the conversation. For her, it is not just, "Give me the point; give me the problem." She is thinking about your past and relating it to certain things; she is watching your body language and listening to your tone. She is taking in all kinds of signals.

So your approach with a male client may need to differ from your approach with a female client. You may need to get to the point more quickly with your presentation to a male client. Whereas with a female client, you may need to take more time, be more emotional, relational in your presentation. Men and women are different (as human beings and as individuals). The better understanding you have of learning styles and gender differences, the better chance you have of connecting.

7. Manage your eye contact and posture
Making eye contact is important if you want to connect. Do not stare; you are not a policeman staring

down a criminal. Do not lock eyes and visually beat him down. Just look at him; maintain eye contact. Have you ever noticed anyone gazing at someone who interests him?

Nancy Reagan used to do this. Sometimes the television camera would turn to her while her husband, President Reagan, was making a great speech, and she would be gazing at him appreciatively, supportively. You could see it in her eyes.

You need to look your client in the eyes when you are talking to him or he is talking to you. Give him a positive visual signal by looking at him with interest, support, and appreciation.

Posture is equally important if you want to create an amygdala connection. The amygdala reads body language very effectively, so do not slouch. Sit up (not stiffly) and appear relaxed. Cultivate a good leadership posture. If you are not sure what that is, watch videos or look at photographs of leaders you respect and admire.

Ronald Reagan and George W. Bush are a couple of my favorite examples. Whether you agree with their policies is not the point. These two leaders mastered the body language of confidence. Ronald Reagan modeled his strong masculine walk on his actor friend, John Wayne. Reagan liked the easy, confident grace with which Wayne moved, and he adopted it to create his own signature walk.

Other leaders also walk and move with assurance. Find one and develop your own style. This kind of body language communicates to the amygdala that you are someone to be liked and trusted.

8. Ask informational questions

When you are interviewing someone or giving a presentation (as in my business lunch example) you need to ask him informational questions about himself. He will love this. He will be happy to interact with you when you ask questions about his children or grandchildren; watch him light up.

9. Learn the power of the pause

Know when to stop talking. A friend asked me to watch and evaluate his presentation to a business prospect while they met at a McDonald's restaurant. I discreetly sat at another table and watched. I noted there were at least six different times when the gentleman was ready to agree to the deal, and each time, my friend kept talking. He eventually lost the sale because he never knew when to shut up. He needed to learn the power of the pause.

You also need to know when to pause. Do not be afraid of silence. When you stop, the other person will feel obligated to fill the vacuum, and he will say something that will usually help your presentation. Be quiet long enough and often enough so the other person can be involved in the conversation. This will build a bridge of connection that your amygdala will recognize and confirm.

10. Speak in stories

Always have a story ready. Never make a presentation to anybody, anywhere, without telling at least one good personal story—one that illustrates what you are talking about, one that gives life, energy, and excitement. The amygdala is more story-sensitive than any other part of the human brain because emotions are created by stories.

Telling a story might also help you discern the learning style of your contact. Remember what I talked about in point six of this chapter? Well, to better understand these three styles, look at how each one responds to storytelling. The aural learner will respond to the words and verbal structure. The kinesthetic learner will take notes on the story and possibly act out different parts. The visual learner will visualize your story and turn it into mind pictures. While the kinesthetic person is taking notes and tapping his knee, the visual person is watching you. (He may take notes, but he is primarily observing.) And the auditory person is probably leaning forward, focusing on listening. As you tell your story, pay attention to how your lunch companion reacts. This might give you a clue to what type of learner you are dealing with.

11. Handle objections with courtesy and confidence

Always remember that resistance and rejection are great opportunities. If somebody resists or rejects you, you are receiving an emotion from him. It may be a negative one, but it is real. That person is expressing a genuinely felt reason he does not want to buy into your idea, which gives you a tremendous opening to win him over. You may succeed; you may not. But the opening is only there if he tells you the truth about why he is holding back or why he is refusing you. And that moment of truth is your window of opportunity.

Let me give you an amygdala-based plan for handling someone's resistance and rejection. If somebody has an objection to your idea, business plan, dream, (or whatever you are presenting), do four things:

- Listen respectfully to his objection (argument).

- Acknowledge his objection (disagreement). Tell him, "I see what you mean"; "I understand your point. Or "I appreciate what you're saying."

- Analyze the objection (hesitation). Make comments such as, "Let's see what that means. You've told me you know somebody who tried my idea, and it didn't work. Let's analyze that for a moment." If you have been respectful to him, he will probably let you do this.

- Answer the objection (concern). Something like this might work, "You know, the person you mentioned probably didn't understand what he was dealing with. Maybe he had someone who gave him the wrong information. I'm not going to do that with you."

There might be times when someone will try to arouse hostility. As he rejects your idea, he might want to get a reaction out of you, get you off your game. Do not take the bait. Stay in control. And if someone is bullying you, use the SBAR approach I have been teaching for years.

When someone is throwing objections at you, or he is dominating the conversation or pressuring you, STOP and BREAK eye contact. The moment you do this, he will likely quit talking because he will not know what you are doing. Next, APPEAR thoughtful: Look down (maybe at your notes) and appear to be thinking about something. Finally, RESUME the presentation. You have now retaken control of the conversation. You have stopped his momentum; you are back in command.

Before I go on to the third element of good amygdala communication, let me say one more thing: These eleven points do not only pertain to your business life. Yes, I used the example of meeting a client for lunch to present a business idea; but many will also help you develop a deeper understanding of the people in your life. Be forgiving and generous to those around you. Give everyone the same generous support you want for yourself. Your God-created amygdala can be an engine of loving feelings as you use forgiveness to connect to everyone in your life. Show an interest in people's lives. Most love to be asked informational questions about themselves. They are happy to interact with you when you show an interest in what they care about. And the connection is even easier if you have similar ideas and tastes. Disagreements and arguments will happen, but they do not need to signal the end of a relationship.

Handling objections with respect and love will work wonders, whether you are at lunch with a business associate or playing a game of golf with your best friend. As I have said before, everything depends on how people feel when they are with you, so use these suggestions to strengthen your amygdala connections.

Chapter 7

The Effective Communicator (Part 2)

When you have successfully trained your amygdala to project positive emotions toward individuals, then you are ready to use that training to connect with and influence everyone you encounter. Most people make decisions based on their immediate emotional reaction rather than their long-term logical analysis; so reaching their amygdalae (creating an emotional response in that deep level of the human personality) is vital to getting through to them. All the preparation and connection techniques of chapter six have to do with making the right emotional impression so that individuals will have the correct emotional reaction to you. If they do, they will open their minds to your idea, your concept, or your business model.

And now we come to the third element of good amygdala communication, which is CONCLUSION.

This has to do with creating a response and a commitment to pursue what you have persuaded someone to do. This is such an important part I would like to devote an entire chapter to it.

The Zig Ziglar Corporation, a well-known sales training company, posted on its website that 63 percent of all sales calls (a majority of salespeople) do not ask for a decision, which is why they do not make a sale.

After your presentation, after your business lunch with a prospective client, you must ask him to do something. Nothing is successful and nothing is completed without an action. Ask him to agree to the terms of your business. (It is OK if he says no; you can live with that—just have a backup plan: "Hey, if you can't do it, I understand. Let's talk about it some other time"... and set up a follow-up meeting.) But there has to be a conclusion, so ask.

Remember that your amygdala is sensitive to choice. It knows whether you follow up on your obligations or not.

I have a good friend who is a public speaker. He told me that for years people would come up and say they would love to have him speak at a meeting they were organizing. My friend would say, "Wow, that's great," and never hear from them again. So, he changed his approach. When someone asked him to speak, he would pull out a little notebook and say, "That sounds great; I'd love to. When do you want me to come, and where is it going to be?" After being told the needed information, he would then confirm and commit on the spot. That was the secret of closing the deal, he had said.

So, swallow your fear and ask for a conclusion because SOME action is better than NO action. When you lead someone to a decision (or make one yourself), you engage your amygdala and his. When you give your amygdala leadership, it responds by giving you support.

I have said before that I want you to be an amygdala communicator and persuader. How someone responds to you will determine if he is moved by your presentation, if he is persuaded to agree to your business proposition.

And that, my friend, is what I am talking about: The Art of Persuasion. It is individuals responding in a positive way to what you have presented to them. You want to create a positive amygdala response; you want them to say, "Yes, I will go"; "Yes, I will buy that product"; "Yes, I want to join."

Russell Granger, who taught the art of persuasion, wrote a book titled *The 7 Triggers to Yes: The New Science Behind Influencing People's Decisions,* in which he talks about how to get people to agree to your proposal. Ultimately, you want your amygdala to say "Yes!" to you, and you want others to say "Yes!" to you; so it is helpful to know how to create that yes connection with others.

Here are the triggers of YES:

1. Friendship

I was speaking at an event at Lehigh University. Bobby Bowden (former head football coach of Florida State University) and Tim Sanders (former Yahoo! executive) were also there. Mr. Sanders gave a presentation based on his book, *The Likeability Factor*. He talked about creating a feeling of friendliness toward other people so they will respond favorably to you. (You need to activate your friendship factor to arouse the amygdalae of other people.) Russell Granger talks about friendship being something you convey to others. Friendliness is the difference between a social and a business connection.

Let me give you an example: Imagine that it is Thanksgiving Day, and you have gathered with various family members at your in-laws' house. In the middle of the meal, you look at your mother-in-law, who worked hard on the dinner, and you say, "Susan, you've done a great job on this meal. I calculate that you used about four pounds of potatoes, twenty-two pounds of turkey..." and you go through a quick analysis of all the ingredients that went into the meal. "I estimate you spent seven and a half hours working in the kitchen. At today's restaurant rates (what a cook earns in an average restaurant), I would say you deserve such-and-such compensation for this meal. Here's the check for your per-hour rate. I wanted to make sure I paid you now. Oh, and I've also included a nice gratuity, as they do in all good restaurants. Thank you, Susan, for the meal."

Everybody is now looking at you with a stunned

expression. Your mother-in-law indignantly stands up, takes your check, rips it in two, and walks out of the room. Your wife, in tears, follows her. You look at everybody and say, "What? What did I do? I'm just paying her for what she did."

Now, obviously, what your wife will tell you later is that, "My mother (your mother-in-law) loves us. This is a family occasion. She's not your servant. She's not someone you hired off the street to cook you a meal. What in the world did you think you were doing?"

Well, what you did was impose a marketing connection on your mother-in-law. You treated her as part of a cold, business transaction. She did not want to relate to you in a business-marketing way; after all, this is Thanksgiving dinner. If you had just thanked her for the meal and said, "You're the best mother-in-law in the world," all that work would have been worth it for her. It would have produced exactly what she wanted: a positive social (not business) family response.

There is a difference between creating a marketing and a social connection. If you start your lunch meeting by saying, "John, I appreciate your time. I figure it is worth so much per hour," you make it a business association; and the client will respond in a business way. You did that; you created the marketing connection, and his amygdala secreted chemicals that caused him to see you as a business contact, not as a friend.

But if you start your appointment by relaxing and

talking about his kids or his favorite sports teams, then you become less intimidating and more like a friend. He will relax and be more receptive to your presentation, idea, or proposal.

Studies have shown that if you like a doctor, you are less likely to sue him for malpractice because your relationship with him has a social base, not a business or marketing one. The moment you have a marketing connection with others, it becomes all business because you can easily dehumanize them. (This is why it is easier to be harsh with people on social media. Since you are physically removed from them, there is no opportunity to form an emotional bond through their amygdalae, which is where social connections are made.)

The amygdala knows the difference between a marketing connection and a social connection. It creates warm, fuzzy feelings for those who are perceived as friends, which is why it is so important to show friendship. If they think of you as a friend coming to share something with them, their reaction will be different toward you. (I am not saying be unprofessional in your presentation, organization, or approach. You can be both professional and friendly at the same time.)

That is what I believe Granger is driving at when he says the first trigger to yes is *friendship*. Be friendly. Create a friendly feeling. Remember, the amygdala is all about feelings, all about being emotionally connected to what is happening.

2. Authority

Russell Granger is talking about finding supportive information to back up your presentation. He uses the word authority, but I think you could also use the word credibility to describe what he is saying.

Sigmund Freud, the father of psychoanalysis, had a definition for authority: he called it source credibility.

Sometimes you need to go to an outside source to create credibility; sometimes you need to use borrowed authority. Let's say you have a new neighbor, and you want to make a positive social connection. You know the two of you have a mutual friend, Phillip from next door, who is a local store owner; so you say, "John, I'm so glad you agreed to meet with me today. Phillip talked to me yesterday and really bragged about you." You borrowed Phillip's credibility, his authority: He is a store owner. He lives next door. John knows him. Authority (in this context) is something you borrow, something to which you refer. It does not mean you are throwing your weight around. You are simply borrowing someone else's credibility (authority) to bolster the persuasiveness of your position, your presentation. You are quoting experts.

The amygdala is easily aroused, so when someone becomes suspicious of you, it quickly cooperates to supply confirming emotions. When you borrow credibility, you reassure the person's amygdala that you can be trusted. So quote people you have already shown your business to. If someone has already bought into your business plan, say, "Ralph down the street has already signed up with me, and he's very excited." You are using Ralph's decision to buy into your business to add legitimacy to your proposition.

3. Consistency

People want to see themselves as consistent, so you can increase your connection with them by reinforcing this desire. I had a situation where a part failed on my car. When I went to a local mechanic to have it repaired, he replaced the part and then said, "Ron, did you realize the car manufacturer issued a recall and was supposed to fix it for free? Did you ever get a notification?"

"No," I said, "I don't remember getting one."

"Take this part, go to the dealer, and say to him, 'There was a recall for this part. I did not get a notification and had to pay for the repair.'"

I went to the dealership, and after explaining the situation, I said, "Joe, you've always taken care of your customers. I have watched you do everything you can to make sure a customer is happy. Here is the part and the receipt (close to $400) for the repairs I just received. Can you help me?" He agreed to take care of my problem.

People want to see themselves as consistent, so when I mentioned to Joe that he took care of his customers, I touched his amygdala and created a positive response.

He was very willing to help me because he wanted to be consistent with my image of him and his image of himself. He wanted to live up to my statement, "You take care of your customers."

The way you frame a question, the way you approach a discussion will determine if people will say yes to you. If you do it correctly, people will want to agree with you to be consistent with how you describe them because they have already agreed that they are the person you say they are.

In your business lunch, you already said, "John, you're the guy who likes to make money. Would you like to make more?" His answer will be, "Yes!" because you described him as a guy who wants to make money. He likes that, so he will want to live up to your assessment. You created a situation where his amygdala agreed with you. That is what is meant by consistency being a trigger to yes.

4. Reciprocity
People respond to gifts. I read about a man who could not persuade a CEO to grant him an interview. No matter what he did, he could not get the administrator to see him. So he came up with a plan: He asked around and found out this executive liked Chinese food for lunch. The man arranged for a local Chinese restaurant to deliver an entire lunch to the executive. The next day, he called to ask the CEO if he liked his Chinese lunch. "No, the restaurant sent the wrong food. I didn't like what it sent," he was told.

"No problem," said the man. The next day, he had the restaurant deliver a different menu, one the executive said he liked. When the man called a day later, the executive started laughing; the man got his interview— and the job.

Gift giving works. People feel an emotional obligation to respond with an open mind if they have been given something. If I am shopping (let's say for a car) and the salesman offers me something to drink, I will not take it, because if he gives me something, my amygdala sees him as a friend and gives me positive feelings toward him. His gift creates a psychological advantage (for him) that causes me to want to do something for him in return. Your amygdala works that way as well. Your emotions are a big part of this law of reciprocity. Doing something for others is a trigger for them to say yes to you.

5. Contrast

When you want to encourage people to say yes, you need to show them how things would be better if they did say yes. In the case of your lunch appointment, show your client a contrast between things as they are and things as they could be if he were to try your idea, concept, or business model.

6. Reason

Provide people with a good reason they should say yes. Do your research to determine what will motivate them to say yes. Remember that people make decisions based on emotion more than logic, so connect your case to their emotions. This involves the amygdala and gives you an opportunity to create emotional support for your argument.

Russell Granger tells the story of a man who tried for months to schedule an appointment with another executive who lived in California. The West Coast executive repeatedly declined the appointment—until the first man sent him a message saying he was going to Hawaii and would be stopping in Los Angeles. Since he would be in the area anyway, could he come by to see him? Because this was an acceptable reason, the executive agreed to the meeting. The first man got what he wanted by offering a reason that caused a positive emotional response.

7. Hope

Give people hope. Give them a possibility for their future. (Yes, this is similar to the Contrast trigger I discussed earlier, though it goes beyond what you offer.)

Hope is a powerful stimulator to the amygdala. When people are convinced that something is possible, their amygdala is stimulated to provide support. "You know, this could work for you"; "This is possible for you"; "This could alter your situation." So, if you give them a reason to believe something could create a positive future for them, they are more likely to consider your idea and say yes.

Dr. Robert Cialdini in the *Harvard Business Review* says, "No leader can succeed without mastering the art of persuasion."

The American Management Association came up with a survey of what it considers the top ten skills for business success. I only want to highlight the first two: the ability to communicate effectively and the ability to inspire and motivate other people. It is not enough to have a great idea or concept. If you want to succeed, you must persuade others to believe in you and in your ideas. This, again, is where that tiny part of your brain, the amygdala, makes an impact.

Chester F. Carlson—physicist, attorney, inventor, and research engineer—had a new idea: a copying machine. In 1934, on his own time, he set out to invent an easier way to copy documents. After countless hours and experiments, he and his assistant finally made a breakthrough in 1938. They made the first xerographic (as his method was called) copy. He tried to interest someone in developing his invention, but over twenty companies turned him down.

Finally, in 1947, the Haloid Company got the commercial rights to xerography, and in 1959 offered the first copiers for sale. Haloid took his idea, changed its name to Xerox Corporation, and created a revolution.

Chester Carlson invented photocopying, but for many years he could not sell his idea to anybody. He later said the reason was simple: He was not a persuader. He could not get his idea across. You can have the greatest dream in the world, but if you cannot get people to follow you or help you with it, your idea will not go anywhere. You will not get your rocket off the ground.

Jack St. Clair Kilby is famous for patent number 3643138. For forty-two years, he could not get anybody to back his invention; he was not a persuader either. He had a phenomenal idea. In fact, it was so good he received the Nobel Prize for Physics in 2000. It was so good there are two trillion applications of his idea in the marketplace right now. Over forty years ago, unable to convince anybody he had something worth developing, Jack St. Clair Kilby invented the microchip. Your cell phone, iPod, and laptop all work with microchips.

Yale University published a list of what it found to be the twelve most persuasive words in the English language. Here is the list in reverse order:

12. Guarantee

11. Proven

10. Discovery

9. Love

8. Safety

7. Easy

6. Health (or Healthy)

5. Results

4. New

3. Save

2. Money

1. You

All of these words arouse the amygdala. They create thoughts and images that cause it to release the emotions that support those thoughts. When you use them, you connect to the amygdala of those people who listen to you. If the two inventors had understood these words and the role of the amygdala, they might not have missed such amazing opportunities.

I want you to be a great persuader. I want people to say, "Yes!" to you. I want your deepest desires and dreams to become possible. This can happen when you train your brain (especially the amygdala) to cooperate with your pursuit of success.

Success is built on your ability to persuade people to follow and support you. And that ability is based on your use of emotion through the deep limbic system of the brain to relate to others and cause them to trust and like you. Think of your amygdala as a guardian, a gatekeeper, who is always on duty protecting your interests. When you understand and train your amygdala, your guardian works for you.

The same is true for everyone you meet. Each has his own amygdala guardian that is constantly evaluating you. When you persuade his amygdala you are trustworthy and likeable, a relationship is born and a door opens to new possibilities.

Everything great in my life has happened because someone persuaded my amygdala, which then created an emotional response that led to a decision:

- My mother painted a beautiful picture of the world of books. She reached my amygdala, roused my emotions, and made me a lifelong reader and learner.

- My father challenged me to be manly and strong and to use that strength to take care of other people. He reached my amygdala, pulled out my emotions, and made me responsible.

- A godly pastor inspired me to invite Jesus Christ into my life as my Lord and Savior. His presentation of Jesus's death and resurrection persuaded my amygdala to release the emotions that led to my decision to follow Christ.

- I persuaded an awesome young woman to let me love her. I connected with her amygdala, and her love connected with mine. My emotions were engaged; I decided to marry her, and she (and her amygdala) agreed.

Amazing things can happen when you train your brain.

God bless your journey!